Patricia Lynch

Storyteller

First published in 2005 by Liberties Press
in association with Cork City Libraries

Liberties Press | 51 Stephens Road | Inchicore | Dublin 8 | Ireland
www.libertiespress.com | info@libertiespress.com
Editorial: +353 (1) 402 0805 | sean@libertiespress.com
Sales and marketing: +353 (1) 453 4363 | peter@libertiespress.com

Trade enquiries to CMD Distribution
55A Spruce Avenue | Stillorgan Industrial Park | Blackrock | County Dublin
Tel: +353 (1) 294 2560
Fax: +353 (1) 294 2564

Sales representation by Compass Ireland Independent Book Sales
38 Kerdiff Avenue | Naas | County Kildare
Tel: +353 (45) 880 805
Fax: +353 (45) 880 806

ISBN 0–9545335–9–3

2 4 6 8 10 9 7 5 3 1

A CIP record for this title is available from the British Library

Cover design by Liam Furlong at space.ie
Set in 11.5-point Garamond

Printed in Ireland by Colour Books
Unit 105 | Baldoyle Industrial Estate | Dublin 13

PATRICIA LYNCH

STORYTELLER

PHIL YOUNG

for Keith

*

Cork City Libraries has supported this publication
in memory of the late Pat Egan

CONTENTS

ACKNOWLEDGEMENTS

I would like to put on record my gratitude and thanks to the following people, who provided me with enormous help in my research into the background and creative works of Patricia Lynch: Eugene and Mai Lambert, who knew Patricia Lynch and her husband Richard M. Fox, and who were so kind to Patricia in her final years; Robert Dunbar, who shared his knowledge of children's literature with me; the archivists of the special collections in the National Library of Ireland; the Munster Literature Centre in Cork; Stella Cherry of the Public Museum in Fitzgerald's Park, Cork; Celia Keenan of Saint Patrick's College, Drumcondra, Dublin; Tom Mullins and Eibhear Walshe of University College Cork; John Quinn, journalist and broadcaster; Mary Sweeney of the RTÉ archives; Professor Eilean Ní Chuilleanáin, Amanda Piesse and Eve Patten of Trinity College Dublin; Siobhan Parkinson, author; Thomas McCarthy, poet and assistant director of Cork 2005; Muriel Ryan, Theo Snoddy, James Gorry and Nicola Gordon Bowe, who shared with me their knowledge of the artists used to illustrate Patricia Lynch's works; Jonathan Williams, Olivia Hamilton, Gwenda Young and Seán O'Keeffe, who gave me such constructive advice on the preparation of the manuscript; and my friends in the South Dublin Writers' Group, who encouraged me all the way. My very special thanks go to my husband and family for their unfailing patience, help and support.

*

Introduction

Patricia Lynch is one of the main reasons that I became a writer. I grew up in Newbridge, County Kildare, during the 1940s and, like many of my friends, lived on a literary diet of Enid Blyton. Then, one dark, rainy Saturday, I arrived at the children's library to find it about to close and all the Blytons gone. Mr Connolly, the librarian, pressed a book into my hand with the assurance that I would like it – and went home to his dinner.

By the time I had eaten *my* dinner, the rain had become a heavy downpour. The book turned out to be *The Turf-Cutter's Donkey* by Patricia Lynch. What, no flashing lighthouses, underground passages, caves, snarling villains or pantries of easily 'borrowed' meat pies? Instead, I reluctantly entered the world of Shamus, Eileen and Long Ears and found, to my amazement, that they lived in a world that was, in many details, similar to my own.

The bog was down the road from our house. Turf-cutters came into town with their donkeys and carts. Their wives sold chickens and butter and eggs. I went to school with children like Eileen and Shamus. In the course of one wet afternoon, I realised that the place that I was growing up in was a suitable place for all kinds of stories to be set in. It was an experience that many of us, writers and readers, have shared over the generations. Patricia Lynch had given us Ireland as a place of mystery, magic and excitement.

Later, as a publisher with the Children's Press, one of the most gratifying things that I ever did was, in the 1970s, to reprint

A Storyteller's Childhood and *The Grey Goose of Kilnevin* in their original format, with the original illustrations.

But who was Patricia Lynch? Small and fine-boned in appearance, she spoke with an English accent. Her formative years were spent outside Ireland. One of her first visits back to Ireland was to report on the aftermath of the 1916 Rising – a task that she undertook with the skill of a well-bred Mata Hari. She and her husband, R. M. Fox, were nicknamed 'The Little Foxes' and were very much part of the theatrical and cultural scene in Dublin. Yet Patricia herself seemed to get very little of the personal acclaim that she so richly deserved as the original, creative force behind modern writing for children.

This timely and long-awaited biography of many people's favourite writer will surely see Patricia Lynch given the attention that, on so many levels, she deserves. Our gratitude to Phil Young for undertaking the task.

Tony Hickey

PART ONE

1

The Background

Once upon a time, in a city in the south of Ireland sometimes called the real capital, was born a little girl who was to become one of the great storytellers of her age, and whose novels are widely considered to be classics of their kind. The city was Cork, and the little girl was Patricia Nora Lynch.

Cork, city and county, is an area that is rich in culture and history and has produced many great writers. The city itself is a very special place which leaves an indelible mark on all who know it intimately. Robert Gibbings, the writer and engraver, himself a Corkman, born just five years before Patricia Lynch, remembers the Irishman at London's Euston Station who asks the ticket clerk for a ticket. 'Where to?' asks the clerk. 'To Cork, of course! Where the divil else!' replies the man.

According to Gibbings, Cork is 'the loveliest city in the world. Anybody who doesn't agree with me either was not born there or is prejudiced.'[1] Patricia Lynch would have endorsed those sentiments. Despite the fact that she lived there for only a short time, she loved Cork passionately, and saw it as the 'dream city of her youth'. She used it as a point of reference for many of her novels and short stories.

The city is indeed a dream city. The name 'Cork' comes from the Gaelic word Corcaig, meaning 'a marsh': the city is built on islands in the marsh. The main street, Patrick Street, curves to follow the winding of the River Lee, giving the city a unique maritime quality. To quote Edmund Spenser:

The spreading Lee, that like an island fayre
Encloseth Cork with his divided flood.[2]

Though Patricia was eventually to settle in Dublin, she always maintained that there was no city in the world to equal Cork, because 'once Cork gets a grip on the heart of a child, it can never be loosened.' She long harboured an ambition to live in Blackrock Castle, which held a strong fascination for her since she first saw it as a small child, and which she describes as 'A tiny castle . . . like a forgotten toy . . . the rushing tide swirling against its white walls.'[3] This romantic, turreted structure appealed to her imagination, and its fairy-tale image remained with her throughout her life, surfacing in her fiction time and again.

On 4 June 1894, in a house in Sunday's Well, Nora Lynch gave birth to a daughter, Patricia Nora, her second child. Nora and her husband, Timothy Patrick, were distant cousins, part of the Lynch clan, which had a smattering of Spanish blood in their veins, possibly dating back to the time of the Spanish Armada. The house in which Patricia was born was a big house with a walled garden, overlooking the city, with its many church towers and steeples, and within earshot of the famous Shandon Bells. It was an indication of the family's financial status at that time that they should be living in Sunday's Well, an area which mostly housed the emerging Cork merchant class. Their fortunes changed owing to a downturn in their financial situation, however, and at the age of three Patricia experienced the first upheaval of her life, when she, her mother and her older brother, Patrick Henry, had to move out of their home and take up residence in Grandfather Lynch's house in Fair Hill.

An air of mystery surrounds the breadwinner of the family, Timothy Patrick Lynch. He was a journalist who had spent many years in Egypt, where he edited a newspaper for a time. At some point while he was in Egypt, Timothy Lynch switched career paths, because in the certificate of his marriage to Nora he is described as a stockbroker. His business affairs appear to have been something of a disaster, and when he died in Cairo in 1900, he left behind him many debts. A letter to his 'Nora darling' in the late 1890s tells her that he was ill with 'desert fever', and soon after this his friend and business partner, Steve Blanchard, wrote to inform the family of his death.

The downturn in Timothy Lynch's financial situation owing to his business dealings left Nora and her two children in a precarious situation. They had to leave the house in Sunday's Well and move in with Nora's father – Patricia's grandfather – Tighe Lynch, an imposing figure of a man who 'wore a long black coat, with a cape, buttoned all the way down, and a top hat tilted to one side.'[4] Grandfather Lynch was a scholar in the old Gaelic sense of the word. He had been a Fenian in his young days, but his wife, who came from a 'Big House' close to Sunday's Well, would have no truck with rebels of any description. He taught Latin, Greek and Irish to those youngsters who craved knowledge but had no money to buy it, and he was also in the process of writing, in Irish, a poetic history of Ireland. It is not known whether this history ever saw the light of day, but we do know that the family pinned their hopes on it bringing them all fame, fortune and a rosy future.

This old man, with his wealth of knowledge, stories and tales, was a vital influence in shaping the mind and imagination of his little grand-daughter Patricia. He surrounded himself with books, and spent every spare penny he had on dusty old volumes which he picked up in second-hand bookshops – of which there were many at the time – along the quays of the River Lee. He boasted that he had never passed a bookshop or a beggar in his life. Patricia was somewhat in awe of this man, with his shaggy eyebrows and stern eyes, but he was a kind man, always willing to help a neighbour in distress. He was nevertheless very much the head of the household. He set himself apart from the motley collection of family members under his roof: he was the only person who entered by the front door of the house – everybody else 'stumbled by the broken steps to the yard and the kitchen', Patricia relates[5] – and he reserved the best room in the house for his bedroom and the second-best for his study, and nobody questioned his right to do so.

The house on Fair Hill was quite a comedown from the big house in Sunday's Well. Fair Hill was a much poorer area of Cork, with the houses climbing higgledy-piggledy fashion up from the North Quays, where the apple women sat with their baskets of fruit, past the dark little hucksters' shops, which sold all kinds of groceries, from fruit and vegetables to tea, sugar and tinned goods, and on beyond Fair Green, which had once been the heart of the area. The house was dark and narrow, and leant precariously towards the city. When the wind blew up from the sea, the windows rattled, the doors shook, and the slates slid from the roof. Patricia gives a vivid description of how on stormy nights she would shiver in her little attic room and wonder if the house would be 'blown down the river and out across the great harbour to the ocean.'[6]

Grandfather Lynch, though a widower himself, was surrounded by women. There was his daughter Kattie, who baked, cooked and scrubbed all day long, all the while dreaming of the day when she would have saved up enough money for her passage to America. There was Hannah, whose talent was haggling for bargains in the stalls along the quays, and who, in spite of her rosy cheeks and laughing face, was malicious and a little trouble-maker, or so Patricia thought. There was Mary, a twin of brother Liam, described by her sister as being 'a half-person', and then there was Patricia's mother, Nora, a talented lacemaker who made yards of lace 'fine as spiders' webs' and sang ballads and recited poetry to Patricia while her steel crochet hook 'flashed in and out like a fish.'[7] Sitting on the big chest in the hall beside her mother, Patricia immersed herself in tales of heroes and heroines, of romance and tragedy, of Ireland's glorious past. The chest itself was a focal point for these stories, as it had belonged to Uncle Henry, who had been lost at sea in a storm off the Algerian coast. It had later belonged to Patricia's father, who intended to take it with him to Egypt but found it too cumbersome. When Nora ran out of poems and songs, she weaved stories about this chest; Patricia responded eagerly to these tales and their link with the father whom she had never really known.

Grandfather Lynch had three sons, Tim, Liam and Cathal, but only Liam lived in the house in Fair Hill, where he shared a room with Patrick Henry, Patricia's brother. Liam was a betting man, following the horses and the races, and money seemed to trickle through his fingers. He had no aspirations to accumulate learning, or to pursue any particular career. Grandfather Lynch pinned his hopes on making a scholar out of his grandson. Patrick Henry himself had dreams of going to university and of becoming as learned as his grandfather, but to become a college graduate took money – much more money than that which arrived periodically in the square foreign letters with the exotic stamps. These letters from Egypt were eagerly awaited by Nora and her son and daughter. They would linger over every word, and carefully count out the notes, which were intended to buy Nora silk dresses and diamond earrings, to get Patricia a doll with real hair and eyes that opened and closed, and to put Patrick through college. Sadly, there was never enough money for any of these things, and the only education Patrick Henry got was that which the Christian Brothers imparted to him.

The house on Fair Hill was always open to friends, neighbours, tradesmen and salespeople, all of whom used to stumble up the rickety steps to the back door and settle themselves in the kitchen to drink tea, talk and exchange stories. Patricia listened in, absorbing all manner of strange tales and turning them over in her mind. One of these visitors was to become the most important figure in the shaping of her storyteller's imagination. This was a *seanchaí,* or traditional storyteller, called Mrs Hennessy, who came from a remote rural area west of Bantry in west Cork and was reputed to have been born with a special gift, passed down to her from her father. This was the gift of storytelling, and the remarkable ability to memorise the great sagas of Ireland's noble past. Mrs Hennessy's periodic visits to the Lynch household were eagerly anticipated by everyone. Patricia describes how, as soon as the *seanchaí* sat down by the fire, 'flinging back the hood of the pleated black cloak that all the older women of west Cork wore, and turning up the skirt of her dress to prevent the fire scorching it',[8] the neighbours would begin to appear. There was Mrs Foley from down the road, there was the turf man, there were the Reillys from next door, there were the two young men who had been sidetracked from their Latin lesson with Grandfather Lynch, and of course there was the Lynch clan. Nora Lynch sat beside Mrs Hennessy, ready to top up her tea and keep her plate filled with the hot buttered potato cake that the old lady loved. The atmosphere was expectant, even tense: not a word was to be missed.

The background to this deep love of oral storytelling was complex, but the love itself has long been a feature of Ireland's cultural past. Douglas Hyde, in his lecture 'The Necessity for De-Anglicising Ireland', which he delivered in 1892, said that the soul of the nation lay in the Gaelic-speaking peasantry. W. B. Yeats also believed that the Celtic past had to be retrieved in order for the nation to assert and define itself. This Celtic revival sparked off a powerful interest in Irish folklore. Yeats saw folklore as the genuine voice of the Irish people. Collecting songs, ballads and folk tales became an important way of preserving Ireland's past, and of lifting the nation from the apathy and depression into which it had sunk following the Famine and its aftermath.

Mrs Hennessy the *seanchaí* was an important link in the chain between Ireland's Gaelic past and the Irish Renaissance associated with W. B. Yeats, Maud Gonne and others. Folk memory, oral storytelling, ballad singing and the recitation of poetry were all part of peasant culture. Just as in the past, the *filí* (poets) and bards of the Gaelic courts had been respected and revered for their skills, so in rural Ireland, in particular, Mrs Hennessy and her like were held in very high esteem.

Storytellers like Mrs Hennessy and her kind possessed a veritable storehouse of ancient knowledge. As Patricia Lynch observes in her autobiography, *A Storyteller's Childhood:* 'The people who lived in Ireland before the days of history were as well known to Mrs Hennessy as the neighbours in her village.' [9]

Mrs Hennessy's visit to the house in Fair Hill was to have

profound implications for Patricia. Not only did she provide the little girl with a deep draught of Irish culture and a link with Ireland's past through her storytelling, but she was also destined to be her travelling companion on a journey which was to be the first of many in Patricia's nomadic life.

2

THE WANDERING YEARS

Patricia was five years old when the long-awaited letter from Egypt arrived in Cork. The family was to travel to England, and from there they would make their way to Cairo to be reunited with their husband and father, Timothy Patrick Lynch. The house in Fair Hill hummed with excitement as Nora packed the big black sea chest, Patrick Henry gathered together his best books and his few personal belongings, and Patricia, with the help of Aunt Kattie, tied up her best clothes and her favourite rag doll, Poosie, in her red shawl. Patricia then sat on the trunk, her picture book under her arm and her bundle beside her, and waited.

Emigration, which had been an integral part of Irish society since before the Great Famine of the 1840s, had by this time reached unprecedented proportions. By 1890, there were three million Irish-born people living overseas. Emigration was accepted as a necessary evil, and in many parts of the country was even regarded as desirable on economic grounds, as those who had made the journey from the old country to the new world sent back not just glowing accounts of the prospects and lifestyle in their adopted lands but also substantial sums of money. This money provided passage fares for young men and women to join their older siblings, as well as ensuring an above-subsistence-level income for elderly parents.

Hardly a family in the land remained untouched by the phenomenon of emigration; it should be noted that women as well as men emigrated. Between 1876 and 1921, 84 percent of Irish emigrants ended up in the United States, with 7 percent heading for Australia and only 8 percent for the United Kingdom.[1] The railways, the factories and the mines needed large amounts of labour and often provided employment for those seeking work in the United States. Subsidised passage rates and a strong support system from established Irish communities ensured a steady flow of hopefuls heading west. Later, as the Irish emigrants gained in confidence and in literacy, they moved from the more menial and manual sources of employment into the police force, nursing and, eventually, the civil service.

Although the emigrants in many cases thrived, they frequently had a strong sense of displacement, placelessness and exile. The longing for the mother country persisted, surfacing in the emigrants' songs and dances. There was a reluctance on the part of the emigrants to identify completely with their adoptive countries; this fact made complete social integration of the migrants difficult. Here, the Catholic Church provided very important support for the emigrants, as did religious-run schools, which reinforced the newcomers' strong cultural identity. Anti-Irish prejudice in England tended to strengthen the bond between Irish workers and to ghettoise them to a certain extent. Emigration to America had a finality about it which emigration to Britain did not; the tradition of the 'American Wake' – that sombre gathering where prospective emigrants were given a send-off similar to that accorded to a corpse before burial – which persisted well into the twentieth century.

Emigration held no fears for Patricia, though. Her best friend, Dinny Foley, and his family were in the process of leaving Cork and Fair Hill and taking the ship to America, and Patricia and Dinny had had many discussions about the wonderful life that awaited them on the other side of the Atlantic. She was sad to say goodbye to Dinny, but he was going his way and she was off with her mother and brother to join her father. How could she be upset about that? It was not to be, however. What happened next was poignantly described in *A Storyteller's Childhood*.

Nora Lynch came down the stairs to where Patricia was perched on top of the trunk. She gazed at her daughter 'sorrowfully with her big grey eyes.' Then she told her: 'You're too young to be travelling to the other side of the world and we not knowing what's to become of us.'

'You're going without me?' I asked, beginning to cry. 'And me nearly six!'

'I must!' she said. 'I must!'[2]

From that moment on, all the security of Patricia's childhood world was to disappear. She was never again to experience a stable, settled home life, and her rootless, wandering existence was to colour her later treatment of her own fictional characters. Today's child psychologists would possibly describe her childhood as nightmarish, with no secure home background, a haphazard education, no bonding with her father, and a relationship with her mother which was constantly being disrupted. Her childhood was undoubtedly a sad and lonely one but, as in the case of Charles Dickens, whose childhood could also be described as nightmarish, it provided fertile ground for the flowering of her creative genius. Thrown in on herself, she read voraciously and lived in an imaginative world of magic and fantasy. Luckily, she had a happy temperament and accepted whatever life handed out her. No matter what deprivations she faced, she always managed to view the world with a sense of wonder and anticipation, and for her each day brought endless possibilities.

Patricia was to be left behind in the house in Fair Hill, in the care of Aunt Kattie, whose sights were set on America, and Aunt Hannah, who was forever tormenting the child. Aunt Hannah made fun of Patricia's rag doll Poosie, she deliberately made Patrick Henry late for school by hiding his schoolbooks, and she turned bedtime into a terrifying experience for Patricia by threatening her with a headless monster which, she said, lurked in the cupboard on the landing near her bedroom door. This was hardly a caring, loving environment for a parentless five-year-old. Things were to change, though.

Mrs Hennessy, visiting the Lynch household at the time of

Nora's pronouncement that she was leaving Fair Hill without Patricia, drank her tea and observed the scene around her, with the weeping Patricia and the sorrowful Nora. She settled the matter with an unexpected offer. 'The child must come to me if her own are goin' from her,' she declared.[3] This offer was met with disbelief. To think that Mrs Hennessy, the most famous and revered *seanchaí* in the whole of Cork, was going to give little Patricia Lynch a home! This was seen as a great honour, and Patricia was suddenly regarded as the most privileged person in the room. Even the jeering Aunt Hannah was too stunned to make a comment. Patricia herself wasn't quite sure what to make of the offer. She wanted to be with her mother and brother, yet she was proud to be singled out for what she could see was something very special. She stopped crying and began to wonder what kind of a house Mrs Hennessy lived in. Surely something as fine as Blackrock Castle – bigger, even! – with lots of books, and high windows through which she could look up at the stars. Her imagination had already begun to throw up images. By now Nora was smiling as if all her troubles had been solved. 'You should be very grateful to Mrs Hennessy,' she said. 'Be a good girl now.'[4] Nora hugged Patricia, Patrick Henry kissed her, Uncle Liam brought out her bundle, her doll and her book, and that was that.

Patricia was about to embark on her very first voyage. Her mode of transport was to be Moddy, Peadar Keeley's donkey. Patricia immediately fell in love with this patient grey creature, with its long, drooping ears. Donkeys were to be a feature of much of her later fiction, and she was to depict their patient, loving and intelligent natures in many of her best stories. Moddy the donkey was better than any golden chariot on this first journey of discovery. 'Did ye never go travellin' before?' asked Mrs Hennessy as they set off. 'There's nothin' to aquil it, nothin' at all – bar comin' home agin.'[5] A settled home was something which would elude Patricia for the rest of her childhood, but the search for such security would always remain a source of hope and adventure for her.

Patricia sat up beside Mrs Hennessy in the donkey cart, with Peadar Keely at the helm, and the trio said goodbye to Fair Hill. They headed down past the huddle of little houses and hucksters' shops and along the banks of the Lee, with the sound of Shandon Bells bouncing across the rooftops. They passed Blackrock Castle standing proudly at the mouth of the harbour, and then headed out on to the open road. Patricia silently registered that the fairy-tale castle was not to be her new home; she wondered if her home would be something even more grand. Soon they met a shepherd bringing his flock from the mountains west of Berehaven to sell in the Cork market. The shepherd immediately recognised Mrs Hennessy and looked admiringly at Patricia.

'Ye lucky little divil,' he said, ' to be keeping company wid a *seanchaí!* [6] Patricia felt proud to be in such a lofty position, but wished that her mother could be there with her. They then met a cattle drover, who also paid his respects to the *seanchaí,* and later, as the shadows lengthened and the evening drew in, they were confronted by a band of tinkers. In years to come, Patricia Lynch's stories would draw censure from critics for her treatment of the travelling community. But Patricia herself had mixed feelings about these nomadic people. She feared them, and she loathed the way they sometimes mistreated their animals, but she also admired them for their independence of spirit, and the adventurer in her connected with their love of freedom, of travel, of the open road.

This encounter was not her first meeting with this particular group. One morning, with her friend and ally Dinny Foley, she had mitched from the convent school. They had spent the morning wandering out into the country, exploring the great world beyond their street and relishing the strangeness of it all. Their excitement turned to fear when they found themselves on the edge of a tinker encampment. The leader, a tall dark man in tattered clothes and with a yellow handkerchief twisted around his head – and a man who was to surface as a character in many of Lynch's books – threatened to steal the children and bring them with the tribe on their journeying. 'Jump in,' he shouted at them, gesturing towards his covered cart, 'and when the polis come sarchin', don't let the ghost of a sound out of yez.'[7] The two mitchers took off and ran and ran, not stopping until they arrived back in Dinny Foley's back yard. For nights afterwards, Patricia had a recurring nightmare that the tinker had put her into his cart and carried her away.

Now Patricia once again found herself face to face with this particular tribe of travellers. The tinkers' animals blocked the roadway, and poor Moddy had her nose butted by a white tinker horse. The chief remembered the little mitcher, and jeered at her that she must be mitching again. But when Patricia told him that she was going to stay with Mrs Hennessy, his whole attitude changed: like all country people, he respected the *seanchaí*. 'The road is yours, ma'am', he said. 'I'd no notion 'twas yerself, Mrs Hennessy.'[8] He shooed aside his animals and children, and in a most civil fashion bade goodnight to the trio. Peadar the turfman was astonished, and made the observation that a gift like Mrs Hennessy's was worth more than any crock of gold.

The travelling community at this time in rural Ireland was seen as being feckless and lawless, subject to none of the rules by which a somewhat inward-looking people conducted their lives. This fear and excitement is reflected in Patricia Lynch's narratives, though, and as Robert Dunbar observed in his introduction to *Secret Lands: The World of Patricia Lynch*,[9] it is usually the older members of the settled communities who demonstrate their prejudices. The young are more open and welcoming, and more likely to experience a thrill of nervous excitement on confronting these nomadic people.

For Patricia Lynch, this meeting on the roadway, and her earlier encounter with the tinker chief, were to provide rich fodder for her developing imagination. In book after book this character would surface, and though the reader of today may find some of her treatments of the travelling community offensive, they were never more than a reflection of the times, and were firmly rooted in the reality of rural Ireland at a particular time.

It was morning before Patricia arrived at what was to be her new home. They had travelled all night with the little donkey Moddy, stopping only once to break their fast and rest the donkey. Patricia's first impression of the Hennessy household was that it was a musical one. Mrs Hennessy's brother Francis Joseph, who was said to be the best fiddler in the whole of Munster, was playing his fiddle as they arrived in, the lively music floating out over the half-door of the cottage. There also to meet them was Mrs Hennessy's husband, James, who was blind. James ran his fingers over the little girl's face and declared that she was not like her grandfather, Tighe Lynch, but was her father's daughter. Patricia, eager to hear more about her father, learned that he 'was always laughin' an' coaxin' an' wild as the wind . . . who thought the world a gorgeous place.'[10]

The little girl's first days away from her mother and brother were eased by the love and understanding of Mrs Hennessy, who made her feel special and secure, giving her breakfast in bed – a great treat – involving her in the household and garden chores, telling her stories, and recounting details of Nora Lynch's childhood to her. Nora had also for a time lived with Mrs Hennessy, and the *seanchaí* described her to Patricia as having been a lovely child, with sad grey eyes, and skin like milk, but who was always discontented and restless. This discontent was thought to have stemmed from the belief that she had been 'taken away'. To be 'taken away' meant that she had crossed from the human world to the fairy world – something which sounds bizarre to us living in a twenty-first-century Ireland, but which was an integral part of folk culture at that time.

The supernatural world of 'good people' and fairies ran like an undercurrent beneath the everyday world. Belief in it was deeply frowned upon by Church authorities and ridiculed by those in high places, but the belief nonetheless persisted, especially in rural Ireland. In fact, past and present very often co-existed quite comfortably in the Ireland of the late nineteenth century. Fairies or 'little folk' could be used as metaphors for things which could not be addressed directly, or for events which were outside human control. Death, crop failure, disfigurement, mental disturbance – all these, when they could not be explained, could be attributed to interference from the supernatural world. Sometimes babies who recovered unexpectedly from a death-threatening illness were regarded as 'changelings' and were treated throughout their childhoods as being in some way different from their siblings; indeed, these children commanded a certain respect from the old people. Hence, it was thought that Nora Lynch's sadness and discontent were caused by the fact that she had been taken away as an infant to some fairy abode and then returned to the mortal world, where she unconsciously hankered for the other world which she had glimpsed.

Patricia quickly settled down to life in the Hennessy cottage. She relished the openness and freedom of living in the country, running barefoot through the fields, gathering fruit from the hedgerows, helping to draw water from the well and to bring turf from the turf-stack – all the while having her imagination nourished through the stories of the *seanchaí*, the blind James, and Francis Joseph the musician. She made friends with Bridie O'Callaghan, a young girl from the neighbouring farm. Bridie, like Aunt Kattie on Fair Hill, longed for the day when she would have saved enough money for her passage to America – a place which beckoned strongly, offering riches and opportunities to those who were brave enough to make the journey. Bridie felt stifled on this mountain farm where nothing happened, but Patricia, new to the scene, found everything about her exciting. She learned how to churn butter, how to feed the pigs and calves, how to milk the red cow, Molly, how to help with the hay-making . . . and on her way home from the O'Callaghan farm to Hennessys, she discovered the Aladdin's cave that was Judy Leahy's shop. This village shop was magic in the eyes of any little girl or boy:

Dolls sat on heaps of apples, ships sailed across a sea of Peggy's Leg and toffee apples: boxes of bricks, boxes of tin soldiers, boxes of wooden furniture were piled on story books and picture papers. Packets of playing cards mingled with bunches of carrots . . . sugar sticks and brandy balls glistened in tall glass jars . . . packets of tea and cocoa leaned against a great slab of salt.[11]

Judy Leahy's shop was a feast for the senses, and was proclaimed to be better than any of the hucksters' shops in Cork!

One of the highlights of Patricia's stay with the Hennessys was the trip to Bantry Fair. Bantry was a large farming town, as well as being a harbour for fishing trawlers and foreign merchant ships, and the monthly fair was an occasion for trading and socialising for both locals and those who lived in the hinterland. This monthly fair was also a mecca for travelling showmen, pedlars, tinkers and ballad singers. Patricia, entranced by the noise, movement and excitement, kept close to Bridie as they explored the various stalls and stopped to watch the Strong Man and listen to the fiddler playing 'The Old Bog Road', an emigrant song which brought tears to Bridie's eyes. In the crush and confusion, Patricia got separated from Bridie, and she eventually found herself wandering around alone and frightened.

In the middle of all the noise and strangers, she saw one familiar face – the tinker chief whom she had met on the road with Mrs Hennessy, and who had terrified herself and Dinny so much back on Fair Hill. Now she ran to him as if he were one of her family, and begged him to help her. The tinker chief took pity on her, though he was surprised that one of the settled community should come to him for help. He invited Patricia to share a meal with his family, and sent one of his youngsters out to search for Bridie or one of the Hennessys. When the worried Hennessys turned up some time later, they found Patricia relaxed and quite at home with the tinker tribe. She had lost her fear of them now that she had spent some time in their company. The local shopkeeper, on hearing of her escapade, remarked that

'They're a bad lot, tinkers! But they do be good to the childer.'
Bridie was not convinced, however, and retorted that 'they stole
my mother's washing on her.'[12]

This fascination with travellers was to become an integral
part of Patricia Lynch's make-up. She was always intrigued by
their lifestyle, their sense of adventure, and their rejection of any
rooted home base. While she herself longed for a settled home
and family around her, part of her secretly nursed a need to
move about, discover new places and experience the world from
a different angle. Her childhood certainly provided her with
much opportunity for such discovery.

On their return from the fair in Bantry a celebratory *ceilidhe*
was held in O'Callaghan's farmhouse. Patricia, tired as she was,
enjoyed the best in traditional Irish music, dancing and storytelling. She forced herself to stay awake so as not to miss any of
the excitement. It was while she was there, in the midst of the
festivities, that her brother arrived to bring the sad news of her
father's death in Egypt.

Patricia had never really known her father, but her short life
had been lived in the shadow of his exploits. His letters from
various far-flung corners of the world had created an air of
excitement in the house on Fair Hill. Her mother had come alive
as she read them, and when the letters were delayed, her mother
had drooped like a flower without rain. The anticipation of his
return home had always been strong, as had the promise of a
better life when he had made his fortune and would, in Patricia's
own vision, 'come walking in one day, a bag of gold in his hand
and a boy pushing a truck after him loaded with presents.'[13] Now
this dream would never be realised. Though she was unfamiliar
with death, Patricia was aware of its finality. Although she had
been happy with Mrs Hennessy, she longed to return to her own
family. So her little bundle was once more packed up, she waved
goodbye to all her friends and to the *seanchaí* and her blind husband, and headed back with Patrick Henry to the house on Fair
Hill.

Following the death of his father, Patrick Henry had to

assume a responsibility well beyond his years. He was now the man of the house, and from this time onward he took full responsibility for looking after his mother. This responsibility remained with him until his own death, and was something upon which Patricia was to remark many years later. She noted that, in many ways, Nora and Patrick Henry were more like sister and brother than mother and son: Patrick Henry had been born when his mother was very young, so, in a sense, they had grown up together. This often resulted in Patricia feeling left out, and she was sensitive to being regarded as something of a burden to her mother and brother in their elusive search for a new and better life.

Patricia was excited to be back in the rickety house on Fair Hill and was especially happy to be reunited with her mother, though she hadn't the words to tell her how much she had missed her. Her mother, however, was sad and unresponsive, and 'looked different', which made Patricia feel sorry and frightened. The house now seemed alien to her, with her mother in mourning and a dark cloud hanging over everything.

There had been another big change since Patricia's departure. Aunt Hannah, her tormentor, had got married and had moved to a smallholding with her new husband, Michael Keiran. Michael Keiran had long had designs on Hannah and had been wooing her with promises of a 'fine bit of a farm' and a chance to be mistress of her own house. Hannah had treated him mostly with disdain, but, as the saying goes, she wasn't getting any younger; there was no queue of people beating a path to the door for her hand in marriage, and her prospects did not amount to much. So Hannah had finally given in and agreed to marry Keiran. After the couple were married, she had to move to Michael's place in the heart of the country – she who had always been accustomed to the lights of the city, the sound of Shandon Bells and the bustle of neighbours coming and going in the house on Fair Hill.

With the death of Timothy Lynch in Egypt, his widow had to go to London to sort out his financial affairs. His business seems to have been in a bit of a mess, and his business partner, Mr Blanchard, had brought all the relevant papers, documents and share certificates with him to London. It was arranged that Nora, Patrick Henry and Patricia would leave Ireland and travel to London to find out what they were entitled to from Timothy's estate. Before going there, however, Nora and Patricia had to travel to west Cork to say goodbye to Hannah. They travelled on the old West Cork Railway, a picturesque line which had opened in 1849 – and which would be closed down and dismantled amid much protest on Good Friday, 31 March 1961. Dunmanway Railway Station was the nearest stop to Hannah's new abode, and Nora and Patricia alighted there.

Dunmanway was then a fine market town renowned for its associations with its founding father, the haughty landlord Sir Richard Cox, who was drowned in its lake, and whose ghost is said still to haunt the area. The story goes that Cox was planning to give the preacher John Wesley, who was coming to the town on a mission of salvation – and whose religious beliefs were not to the taste of Cox and his friends – a ducking in the lake to scare him. Cox went on a practice run, but his boat turned over, pinning him underneath, and he was never seen again – much to the relief of the locals. He is remembered in rhyme in the following ditty:

'Tis there the lake is, where duck and drake is,
And the crane can take his sweet meal of frogs;
But when the night comes round it, the spirits
     surround it,
For there was drownded Sir Richard Cox.[14]

West from the town of Dunmanway lies a craggy, rocky landscape, where puffs of white bog cotton stand out against purple, heather-clad mountains. It is a harsh, spectacular countryside, but there is little fertile farmland. Nora and Patricia soon found this out for themselves in their search for Hannah and Michael Keiran's farm. On leaving the station in Dunmanway, they asked for directions to the farm, to be told that Keiran's 'dump' was up on the high bog, a three-mile walk from the station – and that there was no transport that would take them there! Some long while later, hot, footsore and bedraggled, Nora and Patricia arrived at the ramshackle wooden hut that was Hannah's new home. Here there were no neat fences or tidy gates, as there had been in Mrs Hennessy's smallholding. Old iron bedsteads formed the barrier between animals and humans, more old bed pieces penned in the hens and fowl, and even the open drain which ran down the yard was bridged by yet another bedhead. Nora was shocked to see where her sister was living, and Hannah, resentful and humiliated at the condition of her home, was in no humour to be friendly. The sisters quarrelled almost immediately: Nora flounced out, pulling Patricia along with her, and Hannah slammed the door behind them.

It would be a long time before Patricia visited the Keiran homestead again, but even that journey, and the scene which followed, provided fodder for her later creativity and eventually surfaced in her fiction.

3

Emigrants

The journey from Cork to London on the old passenger-and-cargo boat was a long and tedious one. The City of Cork Steam Packet Company at this time ran a weekly service between Cork and London, stopping off at Plymouth and Southampton. The steamer left Cork on Saturday and reached Plymouth on Sunday, where passengers could disembark for some hours if they so wished. It reached Southampton on Monday, leaving more time for exploration, and finally arrived in London on Tuesday afternoon. As the journey went on, the sounds of emigrant songs and sad recitations from passengers grew louder and more maudlin. Friendships were forged, histories revealed, hopes for rosy futures expressed and emigrant dreams shared.

The Lynch family could afford a cabin, which sheltered them from the worst aspects of the trip – the noise and the weather – but Patricia spent as little time as she could there. Instead, she relished every moment of the trip, rushing about from cabin to deck, talking to everyone, listening to their stories, and reciting ballads and poems for their amusement. When the steamer docked in Plymouth, the three Lynches disembarked, and Patricia gazed awestruck at what was her first sight of an English seaside town. Her impressions of the scene which greeted her are vivid. The place was 'clean and sparkling, with a lighthouse on land gazing out towards the lighthouse at sea. Sailors swaggered past, fishermen carrying nets, ladies just looking at the shops. There were flower shops and sweet shops and shops with gay new books . . . children with bare legs and sandals carrying painted buckets and wooden spades, or bowling wooden hoops.'[1] Nora bought the little girl a book called *Brer Rabbit,* and then the three of them went to a tea shop where they had meat pie 'with thick jelly and crust that crumbled between my teeth . . . followed by jam puffs so light the flakes floated all down the front of my coat.'[2]

Back on board, they set off for the final part of the journey that was to take them to the mysterious Mr Blanchard, whom they believed to be the custodian of their fortunes. A violent storm blew up, sending Nora scurrying back to her bunk. She was in terror of the boat sinking, and of the family suffering the same fate as Uncle Henry, who had been drowned at sea. Her seasickness was stronger than her terror, however, and she took to her bed, leaving Patricia and Patrick Henry in the charge of the chief steward. Patricia was not the least bit bothered by the pitching and rolling of the boat. She, being 'her father's daughter', as she put it, was quite at home on deck, enjoying the camaraderie, and happy to be a part of what she saw as a great adventure.

By the time the ship arrived at the mouth of the Thames, Patricia was on familiar terms with most of the crew. She had told them all of her father's death in Egypt, of the stash of gold awaiting them in London, and of the friends with whom they were to stay in the city. These friends were the Cadogans, who had been former neighbours from Fair Hill. In Cork, the Cadogans had hit hard times, but no one doubted that by now they were prosperous citizens of their adopted city. Patricia looked forward to her stay in their large London home, where she, Patrick Henry and Nora would be honoured guests for the short time it would take to sort out her father's affairs. Then they would bring their fortune back to Cork, buy back the house in Sunday's Well, and all live there together happily.

It was a commonly held assumption that all emigrants to Britain soon found their feet and did very well for themselves. Sadly, this was not always the case, as the Lynches were to find out when they arrived in London. There was no carriage and no welcoming party there to meet them, just a man called Bill

Crouchman and a cart for their trunks. They walked the short distance through thick London fog until they reached a fruit-and-vegetable shop, outside which cabbages, potatoes and carrots were piled. Through this shop they went, up a narrow staircase, and here was the Cadogan home: one big room with three windows. It was a rude awakening for the Lynch trio, and a humiliating experience for the Cadogans to have their Cork neighbours see the poverty of their surroundings.

'Why did you let me think you had money and a fine home?' Nora asked. Mary Cadogan replied: 'Did ever a letter come to Cork that told of hardship and failure?'[3] She was right: failure was not something to which an emigrant could admit. It was one thing to be poor and hard-up in a land where all your friends and relations were experiencing the same hardships, but since everyone knew that London's streets were paved with gold, some of that wealth was expected to attach itself to those who had emigrated. If such success was not achieved, there was a feeling of shame on the part of the migrants and a need to hide their failure from those at home.

The Cadogans had organised two rented rooms in the East End for their visitors. These rooms, in which they lived, slept and ate, were Patricia's first London home. There was a big room that Patricia and Nora shared, and a smaller one for Patrick Henry. Nora was reluctant to call it 'home', and urged the youngsters not to unpack anything they didn't need immediately, but Patricia was excited by all the strange sounds she could hear in the busy street outside, and the comings and goings of neighbours which she could see from her window. She was more than happy to settle here, knowing that she had her mother and brother with her. 'Where we three are together – that's home' her mother had assured her, and Patricia was content with that.[4]

On her first morning in London, while Nora and Patrick Henry began their search for Mr Blanchard and their inheritance, Patricia was taken under Mrs Cadogan's wing and introduced to some of the local sights. The East End of London, then as now, was an area rich in colour and character. There were shops piled high with foods which Patricia had never seen before and which gave off powerful aromas: Dutch cheeses, Spanish onions, Turkish dates, brown and shining, and long loaves of freshly baked bread, shaped like twisted bananas. There was a fish market where Patricia gazed fascinated at glittering trays of salmon, crayfish and lobster. There were market stalls owned by Jewish traders, carrying dolls of every shape and size, coloured balls, skipping ropes, framed pictures, and rows and rows of cups and jugs. Patricia was greeted by everyone they met, and introduced as the little girl from Ireland. She soaked up the colour and the atmosphere, the smells and the noise, and the rich Cockney accent, which she was to absorb as time went by. She made friends with little Harry Crouchman, whose father owned the fruit and vegetable shop, and was taken to Covent Garden to stock up on provisions.

While Nora and Patrick Henry sought Mr Blanchard, Patricia and Harry roamed wild around the alleys and the docks, eating at street stalls and riding on the backs of carts, hidden beneath sacks and boxes. Nobody questioned their freedom to wander, and as long as Patricia was back in their rooms before her mother returned, nobody asked where she had been or what she had been up to. As a small girl in a strange city, Patricia had an astonishing degree of freedom – her mother being preoccupied with her search for Mr Blanchard. This helped build up a resilience in the young girl which served her well in the years ahead, when home did not always mean the three of them living together. These days probably also established her lifelong love affair with food. With the little Cockney Harry as her guide, Patricia ate on the hoof: pease pudding and faggots, pickled cucumbers, fish and chips wrapped in greasy paper, exotic fruits from the markets. Anything that Harry had, Patricia also sampled – so much so that she began to find Mrs Cadogan's simple food quite tasteless. But she still enjoyed her big mugs of steaming tea at the end of her day's wanderings, when she was reunited with Nora and Patrick Henry.

The elusive Mr Blanchard still hadn't materialised, but the Lynch family fell on their feet when Patrick Henry was introduced to a Mr Forbes. Mr Forbes badly need a bookkeeper, and Patrick Henry, who had just finished at national school, was brilliant with figures. Mr Forbes agreed to employ the boy at a pound a week, and to throw in, rent-free, a tiny gate lodge which he owned, and which overlooked the River Thames. Nora and her children moved into this little house and set about creating a home there. This time they unpacked the black chest, taking from it the books, pictures, rugs and delft which represented home, and arranging them around the four-roomed house. Soon the fire was lit, the kettle was singing, Wolfe Tone, Emmet, O'Connell and Parnell adorned the walls, and Patricia and her family were having their first meal together.

Life in the little lodge by the river was good. Patricia explored by day, and when the evenings drew in, Nora would tell her stories by the firelight. Patrick Henry worked hard for Mr Forbes, and it was decided that he would also study, take exams and eventually train to be an accountant. The widowed Nora came to depend on her son more and more, and he rose to the challenge gladly. The time had come also for Patricia to get some schooling, and Nora enrolled her in the nearest convent school, Saint Winifred's. It was a lovely school, her mother assured her, with lots of other Irish girls studying there, so Patricia wouldn't feel lonely, and the nuns would teach her everything she could want to know.

4

SCHOOLDAYS

Patricia adapted easily to the regime at Saint Winifred's Convent School, and the time she spent there was a happy one. Cousin Kate, a cousin of her mother's, had studied there, and so the head nun had no difficulty in accepting the little Irish girl. She was put into the First Communion class, even though she was only six years old, and there she made friends with a variety of other emigrant children. This part of London was home to many immigrants, and Patricia's class was made up of other Irish and English girls, as well as German, French and Italian girls – the common denominator being that they were all Catholic. Every day she learned her spellings and her sums, and after school she played with her new friends, Mary Bernadette Lynch and Cassie Driscoll, before going back to Nora and Patrick Henry and their house by the water.

Patricia thrived in this secure atmosphere. She made her First Communion, dressed in a white frock and wearing a veil which she had been told had belonged to her O'Neill grandmother. This grandmother had lived in a castle, no less, and so Patricia never felt inferior to any of the other children. She celebrated her seventh birthday while she was in Saint Winifred's, and her mother threw a party for all her friends. Patricia went to special Irish classes and did so well at her studies that she won three book prizes – Hans Christian Anderson's *Fairy Tales,* Daniel Defoe's *Robinson Crusoe,* and *The Arabian Nights.* These books were to be her dearest possessions in the years ahead and helped to nourish her imagination with their richness and colour, and to increase her love of language and literature.

In Saint Winifred's also, Patricia came face to face with a tragedy which affected her deeply. The father of her best friend, Cassie Driscoll, committed suicide after his business had collapsed. Cassie became the subject of a whispering campaign among the other pupils. A note was passed around declaring that 'Cassie Driscoll's father shot himself. He is dead. It is a mortal sin. He will go to hell.'[1] Patricia was shocked at this cruelty, and the incident was instrumental in developing in her a lifelong sympathy for the underdog in society. Eventually, the Driscoll family had to move away and Cassie was withdrawn from Saint Winifred's, but Patricia never forgot her friend. Though the subject of suicide was never broached in any of her books, the stories contain plenty of little Cassies – children who are discriminated against or singled out because of family circumstance. In her stories, Patricia shows great psychological insight into the trauma suffered by such individuals.

When word came to Nora that, back in Cork, Grandfather Lynch had died, it was decided that their time in the little house by the river should come to a close, and that the next phase of their travels should begin. Patricia was uprooted from Saint Winifred's, and Patrick Henry gave notice to Mr Forbes. The family removed their pictures from the walls and packed up their belongings. This time, they headed for Liverpool.

With Grandfather Lynch gone, Aunt Kattie was now free to realise her lifelong ambition to seek her fortune in America. Her brother Liam decided to throw in his lot with her, and with a little help from the money that had been hard-earned by Patrick Henry, they travelled to Liverpool on the first leg of their long journey to the new world. Nora, Patrick Henry and Patricia spent two exciting days with them in the city. It was like old times being reunited with Liam and Kattie. Since Nora had decided that she could not bear to go back to Cork now that Grandfather Lynch was dead, they consoled each other and talked and reminisced far into the nights. Then it was time to wave goodbye to Kattie and Liam; they were never to meet again.

The search for Mr Blanchard was resumed. Money was running out, now that Patrick Henry no longer worked for Mr Forbes. The trio travelled from Liverpool to Manchester, from there to Chester, then back again to Liverpool, all the time looking for Blanchard, but still no fortune and still no inheritance was to be found. The family lived in a succession of shabby lodgings in dingy streets. They always seemed to be hungry, and food became an increasingly important element in Patricia's life. She learned to shut herself off from the misery surrounding the family and to retreat into her own vivid world of castles, heroes and places of enchantment.

Nora did her best to turn the rented rooms into a home but eventually became so dispirited that she refused to unpack the trunk at all. 'Insult my pictures and the lovely rug by putting them out in such rooms! I'll not dream of it!' she would declare.[2] And life would become even more miserable.

Patricia grew thin and wan, and developed a cough that she found difficult to shake off. She was also getting no regular schooling, and was falling back on the progress she had made in Saint Winifred's. The Lynches were almost ready to admit defeat when finally a letter arrived from Paris from the mysterious Mr Blanchard. They must come at once, he wrote. He had money and good news.

Mr Blanchard's instructions to them were to come to Paris immediately. Something important had come up regarding their inheritance. Patricia immediately began to spin dreams and fantasies about this exotic French city. She had read about it, she had heard of the magical time Nora and Cousin Kate had had in Paris when they were girls, and now she was getting the chance to go there herself. She would be with her mother and Patrick Henry, and everything would be wonderful. They would be rich, they would live in a beautiful house, and they would eventually return to Cork with their fortune. There was quite another future in store for Patricia, however. Nora decided that her daughter's health was too fragile for any more adventuring. Instead, she was to be sent to a farm in Canterbury in Kent to build up her strength and catch up on her schooling.

Patricia's new home was to be on a fruit farm owned by a Mr and Mrs Martin near a village called Goose Green. The Martins were friends of Mr Forbes, who vouched for them, and they were willing, for a reasonable payment, to take in Patricia and give her a home while Nora and Patrick Henry set off for Paris. So the little girl was put on a train from Canterbury to Ashford, her box of possessions, labelled with her name and destination, with her. From Ashford she was taken by horse-drawn carrier to Goose Green, where she met the Martins, who were to be her family for the immediate future.

Patricia, numb with loneliness, once again closed down her emotions and made the best of the situation. Mr Martin was kind, Mrs Martin was shrewish, Granny Martin saw to it that the little girl was well fed, and Patricia had a friend her own age in Rosalie Martin, with whom she shared an attic bedroom. Rosalie was an eager audience for Patricia's stories and recitations. Patricia discovered a store of books and magazines in the attic bedroom, among them *The Magic City* by Edith Nesbit. This book was to be Patricia's first introduction to an author who was to be a great influence on her life as a writer. Years later, as a young journalist, Patricia interviewed Edith Nesbit and discussed her own writing career with her. The two were to become friends, and Patricia always said that she owed a great debt to the older woman. But for now, Nesbit was her escape route. Her sadness, her loneliness, her disappointments could all be forgotten as she lost herself in the wonderful story of *The Magic City,* a tale of two lonely children who find themselves transported to a magical place where anything is possible. As she read the book, Patricia wondered about the lucky people who wrote stories and drew pictures for books, and she made up her mind that she wanted to be one of them when she grew up.

Patricia started in the village school with Rosalie in the autumn. The work there was not too taxing: schoolwork came second to earning a livelihood in this small community, and the children were released from school to help with the fruit-picking and hop-farming. Every Sunday, the horse-drawn carrier would arrive to take Patricia to Mass in nearby Ashford. There were few Catholics in the district, and none of the Martins were church-goers. Nora Lynch had left instructions that Patricia was to 'attend to her religious duties', however, and this was respected in the household.

Christmas came and went. The little village was snowbound, which gave Patricia plenty of time for reading. She was now twelve years of age, and with Rosalie, she was trusted to travel to the nearest town, where they looked in the shops and had tea in a restaurant. The two girls felt very independent. One day, though, looking for a short cut on the way home, they got lost and ended up spending the night on the marshes. A search party finally traced them, and the two were brought home in disgrace. Worse was to follow. When Nora Lynch heard what had happened to her daughter, she immediately wrote to the Martins, accusing them of gross negligence and informing them that Patricia would spend no more time with them but would be put on the train to London immediately. So once again, Patricia packed up her possessions, said goodbye to the Martins and her friend Rosalie, and set out on the next phase of her fractured childhood.

When Patricia arrived in London, Nora and Patrick Henry, back after a fruitless trip to Paris, were there to meet her. Patrick Henry had by now got a full-time job as a bookkeeper and was earning a substantial salary, so the family could afford to rent a nice house in a quiet suburb of the city. They even had a servant girl to help Nora with the housework. Patricia was dismally behind in her schoolwork, so she was sent to a Miss Lydia, who ran a private school for girls, for special tuition. It was a joyful time for Patricia, being back with her mother and brother, and being part of the family once more. Nora was happy, cooking and baking, telling her daughter stories, and basking in Patrick Henry's success.

But this contentment was not to last long. Once again, Nora became restless. She wanted to visit her cousin Kate and stay with her for a while. It went without saying that Patrick Henry would come with her, but Patricia's life needed more structure, so this time it was decided that she would go to a boarding school. She was to be sent to Saint Joseph's, a Catholic boarding school with a French influence, run by nuns. As it was still summertime, none of the other boarders would be at the school, but that did not deter Nora. Arrangements were made, and soon they were in a taxi on their way to the convent. Her mother rang the bell, and when the door was answered by a lay sister, Nora said goodbye to her daughter and practically pushed Patricia towards the waiting nun. 'This is my little girl, Patricia Nora Lynch,' she said. 'We have to catch a train. Will you take care of her?'[3] With that, Patricia was disposed of, and Nora and Patrick Henry set off to spend time with cousin Kate.

Life in the scholar-less boarding school was a mixed bag for Patricia. The nuns were kind to her and made a special fuss of this solitary child. Patricia, always willing to make the best of things, helped out with the housework, tended the convent garden, fed and played with the cats, and attended Mass in the tiny convent chapel each morning. Night-time was more problematical, because the huge, empty dormitory terrified her. The rows of white-covered beds, the shadows thrown up on the walls, the sound of the wind whistling in the trees surrounding the convent, all set her mind racing and her imagination working. At first, she found it difficult to sleep, but she soon she got used to the strangeness of it all, and would spin tales in her head until sleep came. Here also there was plenty of leisure-time, when she could indulge her huge appetite for stories. By the time September came, and the first of the boarders arrived back, Patricia felt quite at home in Saint Joseph's.

The school was soon bursting with life, and Patricia began to make a new set of friends. There was no slacking here: lessons were tough, the regime was strict, and the food was mediocre, but there was friendship and fun, and Patricia, with her capacity for storytelling, was soon in great demand among the pupils. Since her mother had expressed a wish that her daughter not be given sewing lessons, in case her eyesight might be damaged, it was decided that during the sewing class Patricia should tell the girls stories of an elevating nature. If she knew stories about the lives of the saints, so much the better, but if not, as long as the stories had a moral, then they were acceptable. Patricia would sit on top of her desk, high above the other pupils, and regale them with tales of the Fianna, of Tír na nÓg, and of Saint Brendan the Navigator – the Kerryman who became a monk, and whose seafaring adventures were as exciting as anything in the story books.

Her gift as a storyteller was recognised by the nuns, who praised her efforts and encouraged her to use her imaginative gifts in her writing and essays. When a competition appeared in a magazine for young people for a short story on 'The Life Story of a Daffodil', Patricia submitted her entry. The story won first prize and was published in the magazine, and Patricia was award-ed a cheque for three guineas for her efforts. Patricia Lynch the writer was born. From then on, the dream was always there: one day she, like Edith Nesbit, would be a writer. She would have books published, and all over the world children would read and enjoy her stories. She was still only a girl of twelve, and there were many obstacles facing her, but Patricia was determined that, some day, she would be a professional writer.

By the time the long school holidays came around, Nora and Patrick Henry had returned from their trip and were lodging in an old, reputedly haunted house near Minehead in Somerset. Their landlady was a sea captain's widow and had three grown-up daughters. Patricia relished being with her family once more. She also relished the wonderful food that Mrs Captain Cranley and her daughter Miriam prepared. Patricia consumed vast quan-tities of clotted cream, strawberry jam, cheese tarts, cornflour buns, bread-and-butter pudding – and, Somerset being apple-growing country, cider! She hadn't eaten so well since she had left Cork all those years before, and for Patricia, food was one of life's great pleasures. Her security was once again about to be shattered, however. One night, as Patricia was making her way to bed, Nora informed her that she and Patrick Henry were 'moving on' and that Patricia was to stay with the Cranleys until school term in Saint Joseph's resumed!

Although she missed her family, Patricia by this time was hardened to the idea of separation, and her time with the Cranleys was happy and profitable. The Cranleys were fond of this pleasant and lively youngster. They fed her well, and Mrs Cranley kept her supplied with plenty of writing paper for her to jot down her stories and poems. Patricia was writing whenever she could now; indeed, writing was becoming part of her daily routine. 'I can't stop,' she would tell the Cranleys. 'I like writing better than anything in the world – except reading.'[4] One of the Cranley daughters worked in a newspaper office, and she showed some of Patricia's poetry to her editor. He promptly agreed to publish the poems, and paid Patricia four half-crowns for her work. With her earnings, Patricia bought a second-hand bicycle from the local blacksmith! For the rest of her school holidays, this mode of transport afforded her the freedom to explore the countryside and the tiny ports on the Somerset coast. These new places, new sights and new experiences all provided fodder for her creative imagination – and helped deaden the pain of being once again separated from her family.

When the following Christmas holidays came around, Nora and Patrick Henry were still searching for the elusive inheritance and were once again on the move. What to do with Patricia was again a problem. This time Nora came up with the proposal that Patricia should return to Ireland to stay with her Aunt Hannah and her husband Michael Keiran. Aunt Hannah had expressed a desire to see her niece after all these years. Nora argued that, because Hannah was the only one of the family left in Ireland,

and since 'she always had a *grah* for you',[5] it seemed the right and natural thing to do.

Patricia was shocked. Aunt Hannah had always been her tormentor, and on the one and only time they had visited her since, Nora and Hannah had had a row, and Nora had stormed out of the Keiran home without so much as a cup of tea. Patricia had no desire to visit Hannah. Besides, she would have to travel by boat alone; what if Hannah didn't come to meet her at the port? As always, however, Patricia complied with her mother's wishes. She packed her trunk and was put on the boat for Cork, consoling herself that at least she would be seeing Cork again, and her beloved Blackrock Castle, and maybe even Fair Hill and Mrs Hennessy!

She arrived in Cork in a sleet storm, a returned emigrant among many returned emigrants, lonely and apprehensive. Hannah was there to meet her – the same old Hannah, abrupt, abrasive and sarcastic. The Lynches were gone for ever from Fair Hill, she told Patricia. Patricia's home was with her now, like it or lump it. A tearful Patricia followed her aunt across Cork city to the railway station, to board the train for Dunmanway. It was bitterly cold. She was wet through, numb and miserable. At the railway station in Dunmanway, Michael Keiran rushed forward to greet her. He hugged her, genuinely delighted to see her again, and Patricia felt warmed by his love. At least she knew that Uncle Michael wanted her company and was looking forward to having her in his home. Uncle Michael had no guile in him. He took her box and suitcase and carried them out of the station to where the little donkey, Grey Lad, drawing a creel-sided cart, waited, its head drooping. They set off through the town of Dunmanway, gaily festooned with Christmas decorations and lights, while Michael told Hannah and Patricia of all the good things he had bought for the festival. 'I've biscuits an' sausages . . . oranges an' nuts an' apples an' a barm brack, a monstrous bag of sweets, an' the biggest red Christmas candle in the town!' he declared. 'Tricia's goin' to have a rale hearty Christmas!'[6]

Patricia spent that Christmas in the ramshackle house in the heart of the bog. The Keirans' living conditions had not improved since the last visit Patricia and Nora had paid them. The house had grown haphazardly according to Michael Keiran's whims. Rickety sheds jutted out from the main structure, ropes with rocks hanging on them secured the roof, more rusty bedsteads fortified the surrounding areas, and inside was just as much of a mess. Patricia's room was a monumental act of love on Michael's part, though. Everything in it he had made with his own hands for his young visitor. The bed, the chest of drawers, the chair, the half-made table, all literally strung together for love of Patricia. She was very touched, and this expression of love more than made up for Hannah's surly reception of her.

Hannah was happy to let Patricia do any cooking or housework there was to be done, and even grudgingly said that she would keep Patricia on if she wanted a home, now that she was a girl without a father, and had a mother who was completely wrapped up in her son. This comment hurt Patricia more than anything else. 'She is fond of me,' she declared. 'I'll never leave my mother'.[7] Hannah snorted in reply. She had seen her niece tossed about like a rudderless boat ever since she was a toddler. She was now almost fourteen, well-educated, confident and competent, and Hannah was jealous of how close she was to Michael. It suited Hannah well to have Patricia as her unpaid cook and housekeeper, however; this gave Hannah more time for reading the romantic novelettes which she kept in a sugar box in the kitchen.

With Christmas over, Patricia looked forward to returning to Saint Joseph's, to her friends and her studies. She was still writing: pages of poems, ballads and stories – which Hannah used to light the fire whenever she found them lying about. Writing without an audience or a readership was not ideal, and Patricia longed for the eager reception her stories always received in the boarding school.

But yet another blow awaited her when she asked Hannah what arrangements had been made to send her back to England to resume her education. Hannah looked up impatiently from her novelette. 'How d'ye think Nora can put money into gold mines and send ye to an expensive school as well?' she asked. 'From now on, ye must earn yer keep.'[8] Hannah was right: Patricia had indeed, without discussion or consultation, been withdrawn from Saint Joseph's. Nora and Patrick Henry were still chasing their dream, and Patricia was to be left in west Cork with Hannah, to be a general skivvy in return for her keep.

As always, Patricia accepted her fate without protest. She worked hard at making the run-down cottage into some kind of a home, cooking, baking, scrubbing and running messages. She used her bleakly beautiful surroundings as material for her stories. She read and re-read her collection of books, and wrote poems while gazing at the stars through the lopsided windows in her room. When spring came, Patricia helped Michael out on the windswept bog, piling up the sods of turf that he cut with his slane, stacking them on end to dry, then loading them on to the cart and leading Grey Lad back to the cottage. She also went along with her uncle when he was hired to cut turf for the neighbours, and spent long summer days out of doors, growing tanned and sturdy from the sun, the exercise and the rich bog air. She was friendless and lonely, though: even Michael's kindness to her did not compensate for the fact that she had no one of her own age to talk to, and no mother or brother to confide in.

Just as she felt she could take no more of the loneliness and of Hannah's constant nagging, a message came from Nora. Patricia was to return to London at once, to rejoin her mother and brother. It transpired that Mr Blanchard had finally traced the title deeds to her father's land in Egypt. The family were to travel together to Egypt to stake their claim.

5

GOODBYE TO CHILDHOOD

Patricia boarded the boat that was to take her away from Cork and reunite her with her family. She was happy and excited. She was to see Egypt, the land where her father had lived and made his fortune, and where he had died – the place which had been part of the Lynch family's dreams and hopes for so long. She was to be reunited with her mother. Nora and Patrick Henry wanted her. They were to travel together and claim their inheritance.

She was a little sorry as she watched Blackrock Castle disappear from view. She would have liked to have seen Fair Hill one last time, but what was Fair Hill without the Lynches? With Grandfather dead and the family scattered, it was just a place. She put these thoughts behind her and looked forward to seeing her mother and brother once more. Three days later, the ship steamed up the Thames and docked. She walked down the gangway, behind the man carrying her tin box and her case, and there they were, her mother greyer than she had remembered her, and Patrick Henry, shabby-looking and lacking some of the confident air which he used to have. They didn't want to hear much about how Patricia's life had been but were eager to talk of the golden future which was now within their grasp. New clothes, a new home, adventure, and never again having to worry about money.

The trio stayed in a hotel in London for the next few days, where they ate well and bought all the clothes they would need for the journey ahead. Patricia, no longer a schoolgirl, was fitted out with a smart navy-blue costume, a felt hat, brown shoes and stockings, and a travelling coat with a fur collar. She felt grown up, elegant and loved, and happy to be leaving behind her schooldays and her labour on the bogs of west Cork.

Having seen all the sights of London, the Lynches caught a little steamer to Ostend. From there, the plan was to go to Bruges – where Uncle Henry had spent some time at college before he was drowned at sea – and then on to Verviers, where Nora and Cousin Kate had been at school. Nora wanted this pilgrimage into the past before embarking on the long journey to Egypt. She now had money – an advance on her claim – but Nora and money were soon parted.

They arrived in Bruges and made their way to the tall old house where Nora and Kate had stayed many years before. Their landlady was a Madame Baerasael, who, with her husband, Monsieur Baerasael, and young son, Josef, lived over the wine shop which Monsieur Baerasael ran as a business. On their first night in this dark house, with its shadowy walls and heavy furniture, Patricia became ill. She developed a high temperature and a fever, and was conscious of nothing but the sounds of the many church bells discordantly chiming across the rooftops day and night.

For days, she hovered in and out of consciousness, aware of voices, footsteps and billowing curtains, and always the bells, ringing, ringing. Then the fever broke. She woke up naturally, to find herself propped against pillows in the big double bed. Patrick Henry stood by the window watching her, while Nora crouched with her back to her, packing her suitcase, folding all the new clothes which had been put into the dressing table and the wardrobe on their arrival in Bruges. She stood up as she became aware of Patricia watching her. 'You'll not mind us going, now you're better?' she asked. 'Madame has promised she'll take care of you.'[1] Patricia closed her eyes. She would never see Egypt. They were going away again, and once more she was to be left behind. For her, the dream was over: her mother and brother would travel on to find their inheritance in the land of the Pharaohs, and she was to be left in Bruges with the Baerasaels – whose first language was French, and who had been instructed by Nora to speak to Patricia in French whenever possible, in order for her learn to the language. Patricia voiced no objection and, as ever, accepted what seemed to be the inevitable.

Nora left money with the Baerasaels for Patricia's upkeep, and they looked after her well, even sending her to the local convent school when she felt strong enough to go to school again. Patricia, who did not know enough French to hold her own with the other girls and was obviously not able to amuse them with her stories, described herself as the dunce of the class. After school, she and Josef would explore Bruges together, wandering the tiny alleys along the canals, climbing up the many bell towers, watching and listening to the market traders, and admiring the expensive shops that lined the main thoroughfare. Bruges at this time was an old-world city. The brass- and copper-smiths displayed their wares along the canal banks. The lacemakers worked from their homes, and could be seen sitting in their doorways, fingers darting in and out, needles glistening. Graceful mansions and brick houses with their unique step gables lined the canals, throwing their shadows across the smooth waters. It was a city that was made for exploration by a young girl.

Soon the money Nora had left for Patricia's upkeep ran out. There was no word from Egypt, and no news of gold mines – or anything else. Patricia had to be withdrawn from the convent school. The Baerasaels were no less kind to her, however. They treated her as one of the family, and Patricia reciprocated by helping Madame Baerasael cook and shop, and look after the other lodgers. Autumn slid by, and soon there was another Christmas for Patricia – a very different one from that which she had spent in the desolate west Cork bog, with Hannah and Michael Keiran. Bruges was a truly magical city at Christmas time, and Patricia's imagination went spinning into a fantasy of

51

knights and princesses and haunted bridges, of castles and res-
cues and medieval adventures. The canals froze over, and on the
night before Christmas Eve she and Josef joined the skaters on
the shimmering ice, beneath the December sky, ablaze with
starlight. All around, Japanese lanterns bobbed and flickered, as
the skaters whirled round and round. Carols were sung in the
moonlight. People laughed and greeted one another in Flemish,
and Patricia was caught up in the romance of it all. She herself
couldn't skate properly, but the Baerasaels linked her, and she
was swept along as though she was flying. They returned to the
tall old house, where they drank coffee and ate flaky croissants
and tiny cheeses, and the festivities continued long into the night.

There was only one other boarder staying with the Baerasaels
at this stage. Her name was Miss Carmichael, and she was a travel writer from England. She and Patricia became good friends,
and Miss Carmichael encouraged Patricia to keep on writing.
Patricia confided in this sympathetic English lady, telling her of
her travels, her many 'homes', her loneliness at being apart from
her family – still searching for their gold mine – and her uncer-
tainty about her own future. Miss Carmichael listened attentive-
ly and then gave Patricia a piece of advice which was to have a
powerful effect on her future. 'Perhaps writing will be *your* gold
mine,' she said. 'You should learn shorthand and typewriting.
With them, and a good knowledge of English, a girl can go
through the world.'[2] Patricia thought deeply about this piece of
advice and decided once again that, yes, writing would be her life.

Soon after this, a letter arrived from Egypt. Nora and Patrick
Henry had finally tracked down the Lynch inheritance. It transpired that a cotton factory had been built on the land owned by
Timothy Patrick Lynch and, although there was no gold mine
and no fortune, there was a substantial sum of money awaiting
Nora – enough to pay off the Baerasaels and put Patricia
through college to train to become a teacher.

Patricia was happy that the treasure-seekers had at last
reached their eldorado. She was happy not to be in debt to the
Baerasaels any longer. But . . . become a teacher? No, that was

not for her. Her mind was already made up. She had survived her fractured childhood; now she would learn shorthand and typing and, like Miss Carmichael, go through the world!

"Lan, Children of Lir! But at rouse!"

6

MOVING ON

Patricia said goodbye to the Baerasaels, her friend Josef, and her mentor Miss Carmichael, and set out for London to rejoin Nora and Patrick Henry. Her time in Bruges had given her a new maturity and a certain sophistication. She felt comfortable mixing in any stratum of society, could converse quite well in French, and had a knowledge of good foods and wines. In short, she felt ready to launch herself into the adult world. Nora, however, wanted her education to be more complete, so, on returning to London, it was decided that Patricia would finish her education in the convent day school in Peckham, near their new home. Everything was different now: there was enough money for Nora to keep the family together and, most importantly for Patricia, they were all together again.

Patrick Henry continued with his accountancy examinations, qualified as an accountant, and found no trouble securing positions. He was a conscientious and diligent worker who gave his all, and his skills as an accountant were second to none. The relationship between him and Nora was as close as ever. She was always his first priority, and he was determined to give her all the things she had missed out on early in life. Patricia had long ago realised that she would never have such a close relationship with her mother as Patrick Henry did, and had accepted that situation, though she still had moments of sadness and loneliness. When she did feel abandoned, as always she retreated into the world of her imagination – her secret world, where nothing was impossible and where fantasy and reality existed side by side.

Patrick Henry's work often took him to other cities – Manchester, Edinburgh and Paris – and when he went, he of course took Nora with him. Nora's wanderlust was not sated by the ending of the Egyptian quest. She loved travel and new places; whenever she had to stay in one place for more than a few weeks, she became restless. As Mrs Hennessy had said to Patricia all those years before, Nora had always been a strange, dissatisfied little girl. She loved it when Patrick Henry announced that he had to travel to this city or that, and would be packed up and ready to leave at the drop of a hat. If the trip was to be a long one, Patricia would come too. She would finish up in the school where she was studying and enrol in yet another one in whatever city they would find themselves in. During this time, she went to the Dumfries Academy in Scotland and also lived and attended school for some time in Edinburgh, a city about which she was to write many years later.

Patricia saw these new experiences as more material for her imagination: she was always storing up memories, observing and noting things – but not making new friends or settling in anywhere. She was reading and writing voraciously, and was in no doubt as to where her future would lie. Sometimes the three of them would return to Cork in the summer, and she would relive childhood experiences and catch up on old acquaintances and friends who were still alive, and who, unlike so many of her Cork relations, had not emigrated. Everything had changed: her best friend, Dinny, had died on the journey to America, Grandfather was dead, aunts and uncles had made lives for themselves in the new world. But Cork was still where Patricia felt most at home, and she loved returning there.

When Patricia finally finished her regular schooling, she set about training for what would be her stepping stone to becoming a fully fledged writer. She enrolled in a commercial college in London to learn typing, shorthand and the other skills she needed to get a job in journalism.

This was a period of great political agitation and unrest in London. The question of women's franchise had been foremost in the minds of many since early in the century, and the demand for votes for women was gaining momentum with every passing year. On 23 June 1906, a deputation representing half a million women had met the Prime Minister, Sir Henry Campbell-Bannerman, to press their claims for the vote. This deputation was led by one Emmeline Pankhurst, founder of the Women's Social and Political Union, who told a six-thousand-strong crowd in Trafalgar Square: 'We have been patient too long. We will be patient no longer!'[1] In October of that year, eleven suffragettes were jailed for their part in rowdy demonstrations during the opening session of Parliament.

It was an exciting time and place for a young woman whose senses were alert to the huge dramas being played out around her. The young Patricia Lynch felt strongly the justice of the cause of the Suffragettes, and was full of admiration for the Pankhursts, who were in effect putting their lives on the line in the struggle for women's rights. Patricia was also conscious of the appalling conditions in which so many families in England lived at that time: a report published in 1913 had stated that one in twelve children at state elementary schools was suffering from disease or the effects of poor nutrition. Patricia saw poverty, disease, hunger and slums all around her, and the injustice of the two-tiered society made her very angry. She wasn't the only one. On the labour front, there was much agitation. In the shipbuilding industry, a lockout followed a series of wildcat strikes, and more than one hundred thousand men were affected. There were also labour riots in London, Liverpool, Manchester and other major cities.

As soon as Patricia had finished her schooling, she could no longer stand idly by. She offered her services to Sylvia Pankhurst, daughter of Emmeline Pankhurst, who, as well as campaigning for women's votes, carried out political and social work in the East End of London. Patricia involved herself with the suffragettes by joining the staff of the *Workers' Dreadnought*, a weekly journal edited by Sylvia Pankhurst which claimed to be 'An organ of International Socialism with a Bolshevik Policy. Revolutionary News a Speciality'. Patricia also helped to raise money by organising dances, lectures and meetings. She put on plays involving local children, sometimes writing the pieces and gathering the children around her to play the parts. She had a natural talent for firing the enthusiasm of the children: indeed, she had a childlike enthusiasm herself, and this led her to see each day as a fresh opportunity.

Of all the Pankhurst women, Sylvia Pankhurst was perhaps the most committed to social justice. Her interest in suffragism broadened to embrace socialism, and later communism and anti-fascism. In the years ahead, she was even to get involved in the fight against colonialism in Africa. She was a source of inspiration for Patricia, who was now turning her attention to the social and political injustices being perpetrated across the Irish Sea. In one sense, Patricia was very much a young woman of the East End: she loved the direct, no-nonsense Cockneys and retained their accent until the end of her days. On the other hand, she never lost sight of her Irishness. She was an active member of the Gaelic League, which was committed to establishing an Irish-speaking nation and to fostering Irish culture and customs. She made frequent trips back to Ireland to support the 'Cause'.

With her background and her family history of involvement with Irish nationalism, it seems inevitable that Patricia would come to consider herself an ardent nationalist. 'I was brought up,' she later wrote, 'to think that the best thing I could ever do would be to die for Ireland, and I was simply crazy to do some-thing for the Cause.'[2] She had a romantic notion of nationalism, which she absorbed through stories told to her by her mother and grandfather – a Fenian who had spent some time in jail because of his beliefs. Like Sylvia Pankhurst, however, she was also conscious of the acute social deprivations which existed in Ireland under British rule. In the years leading up to World War I, social and political unrest were very often inseparable. Though the Gaelic League professed to be non-political, it provided a launching pad, as it were, for some of the more nationalistic movements such as Sinn Féin and the Irish Republican Brotherhood, as well as for socialist pressure groups.

In 1908, Jim Larkin, assisted by James Connolly, had organised the Irish Transport and General Workers' Union with the aim of improving the living conditions of the working class. This union had rapidly expanded and become more vociferous. In retaliation, the employers formed themselves into a federation, and in August 1913 Larkin's members were locked out, and twenty-four thousand workers were left without employment. The conflict lasted for eight months – eight months during which there were rallies, skirmishes, baton charges by police, riots, arrests, imprisonments and even deaths. Connolly felt that a military uprising was the only way to free the people, and when war was declared on 4 August 1914, as always 'England's difficulty' was seen as 'Ireland's opportunity'.[3]

Meanwhile, back in England, with the policy of recruitment of women for the labour force and for the war effort, the question of suffrage for women took a back seat. Sylvia Pankhurst was now campaigning for equal pay for women who were doing the work of men, and she was also keeping a watchful eye on events in Ireland. When, in 1916, news filtered through of an uprising there, she turned to Patricia Lynch, asking her if she would be willing to go to Dublin and bring back first-hand information about the insurrection, so that the *Workers' Dreadnought* could give its readers a view of events from the republican side. Patricia felt that now, at last, she had the opportunity of doing something for the Cause. In an article entitled 'Getting the News Across', published in the *Irish Press* many years later, she said: 'Like the Irish exiles in London, I was thrilled when the news came of the Easter Rising. I had not long left school, though I was a member of the Gaelic League and had earlier been associated with Junior Sinn Féin in Cork.'[4]

When Sylvia Pankhurst suggested that Patricia travel to Dublin, Patricia needed no persuasion. She felt highly honoured to be Pankhurst's 'chosen one' and was eager to put her journalistic talents to the test. So, in April 1916, she set out for Dublin on what was to be a historic journey of discovery.

7

GETTING THE NEWS ACROSS

The Rising in Dublin, which began on Easter Monday 1916, took the British by surprise. It did not seem possible that the might of the British Empire could be challenged by a puny army of ill-equipped rebels. Even the nationalist Irish themselves felt that the Rising was a futile gesture, and the rebels were jeered and spat upon by many Dubliners, who were appalled at the wreckage and destruction caused by the insurrection. Indeed, it was obvious that there was more enthusiasm for the rebel cause from the Irish exiles in London than from people in Ireland.

The *Freeman's Journal*, a widely read newspaper of the time, summed up the general feeling when it stated that 'the insurrection . . . was an armed assault against the will and decision of the Irish nation.'[1] Reports in most other English newspapers were equally negative and condemnatory. Sylvia Pankhurst, always supportive of the Irish cause, was anxious to get a nationalist viewpoint on the Rising. She was fired with enthusiasm at the events in Dublin, and indeed at one stage contemplated going over to Ireland to see the situation for herself. Discretion prevailed, however: the view was taken that such a well-known activist as herself would never get past the authorities. In the office of the *Workers' Dreadnought* on Old Ford Road in London, Sylvia Pankhurst, Patricia Lynch and other members of staff discussed the best plan of action. It was decided that Patricia, as a young, unknown Irishwoman, would have the best chance of getting through. So Patricia, now aged twenty-two, and very excited at being chosen to carry out such an important task, disguised herself as a schoolgirl and boarded the train from London to Holyhead. Her well-rehearsed story was that she was going home from school to an aunt in Dublin, to spend the Easter holidays with her.

Patricia joined the throng of soldiers in Euston Station on the first leg of her journey to Holyhead. For security reasons, only single tickets were being issued to Holyhead. From Holyhead, she got the boat; it was again full of soldiers, including one with an Irish accent, who told Patricia that he had enlisted to help the Belgians and that he did not want to fire on people who were fighting for their country. Other travellers complained at the disruption of their Easter-holiday plans, of the difficulty of not knowing whether or not they would be able to travel on to their destinations in Ireland, and of the lack of communications in Ireland. Nobody actually referred to the Rising itself.

In Dun Laoghaire – at that time called Kingstown – a great heap of mailbags was piled up on the quay, because the mailboat service between Ireland and Wales had been suspended. At first, Patricia was told that no civilians were allowed to land, but eventually, with the help of her soldier friend, who claimed that she was his sister, Patricia was allowed to disembark. When she reached Dublin, she found barricades across the streets and the air heavy with the smell of burning and dense clouds of smoke, which obscured the ruins of buildings. Rows of shops had their front windows broken, and goods were scattered among the broken glass. O'Connell Street and Eden Quay were black with dust, and soldiers and police stood along the pavements, preventing people from entering side streets. The General Post Office was peppered with bullets, and bodies were being brought out from the ruins. Patricia felt that she had entered a nightmare world.

Before leaving London, Sylvia Pankhurst had given Patricia a list of contacts, as well as an introduction to a Miss S. G. Harrison, a social worker, who was to arrange accommodation and food for Patricia during her stay in Dublin. One of the contact numbers was that of George Russell (Æ) at his home in Rathgar, one of the city's south-side suburbs. George Russell was a well-known supporter of issues relating to social and political justice and was a great champion of young writers and poets at that time. Patricia duly made her way to Rathgar, but was told that Æ was in his office in Merrion Square. She headed back into the city centre, where she met Æ for the first time. She describes in her article on the Rising how the great man wept openly as he told her that his friends James Connolly and Francis Sheehy-Skeffington had just been shot. Sheehy-Skeffington, a pacifist and a socialist, had been attempting to prevent the looting of bombed-out shops when he was killed by a British officer. As a pacifist, Sheehy-Skeffington had taken no part in the Rising and indeed had condemned what he called 'barbarous warfare' – which made his killing all the more cruel.

In her article, Patricia goes on to describe the suffering of the people of Dublin, especially those women who were searching for their husbands and sons and didn't know if their bodies were still lying in the rubble of the blackened ruins. She describes the scramble for food, the crying of frightened children, the heroism of the rebels, the confusion of some of the soldiers, whose loyalties were divided, and the scenes of utter confusion.

When the time came for Patricia to return to London, she had to go to Trinity College, then held by the British army, to get an official pass. Here she was forced to line up between two prisoners, whom she describes, with an eye for detail that would serve her well in her subsequent career as a children's author, as 'a boy of about seventeen, very thin, poorly dressed but holding his head high' and 'a mild-mannered older man with clumsy clothes and restless hands.' She was then brought in to the officers' room, to be cross-examined about her movements, her background and her political affiliations. Her pass was stamped, and she then had to have it countersigned at Dublin Castle. At Dun Laoghaire, she was again quizzed and her luggage searched. The officials went through all her documents and papers, and asked her if she was bringing back any other material. 'Only this,' replied Patricia, holding up a cheap novelette with a gaudy picture of a foolish-looking girl on the cover. The official waved the trashy novel aside impatiently, never suspecting that between the pages were Patricia's closely written notes of what she describes as 'all that I had seen in that time of Dublin's tragedy and glory.'

When she was safely back in London, Patricia wrote her account of the Rising for the *Workers' Dreadnought*. The article contained a poignant account of a young woman caught up in the violence:

> When the firing began she went out to see if she could help, but was ordered back by the military. All night she remained alone with a dog, listening to the shots passing over the house, and praying for those who were killed. Towards morning she went out, meeting another woman. They went towards Mount Street Bridge intending to search the houses and gardens where the fighting had taken place. They found a young soldier lying on his back, his hands flung above his head as though asleep. They returned twice to him before they could realise that he was dead. Further on they came to a soldier entangled in some wire. They had to cut away nearly all his clothes before they could get him out. Then they found a little Sinn Féiner, barely twelve years old. He was wounded in the head, and his brains were showing. He was still conscious, and his pitiful white face, with its big dark eyes wide open with fear of the soldiers, wrung their hearts. At the women's request a soldier ran for a priest. When he came, the child's face lighted with joy, and his terror vanished, though he was dying.[2]

The article was so sought after that three reprints of the issue were called for. Her article and two others, one by Sylvia Pankhurst and the other by a May O'Callaghan, were later republished in a pamplet called *Rebel Ireland*. W. B. Yeats was most impressed by the authenticity of the voice in this piece of writing. He described it as being the first published account of the Rising written from an Irish perspective, and he brought a copy of the pamplet with him to Paris to show to Maud Gonne. Patricia later met Maud Gonne in London, when she received an invitation to visit the London home of Eva Gore-Booth to meet some of the Irish republican activists living in the city. The invitation was actually addressed to 'the writer of the article', but Patricia and Maud Gonne were very soon on first-name terms, and subsequently became such close friends that they corresponded with each other for more than forty years. In 1922, when Patricia's mother died, Maud Gonne wrote to her, saying: 'I am so sorry to hear of your present trouble. You must feel so lonely without your dear mother.'[3]

In 1918, Maud Gonne, Hanna Sheehy-Skeffington (the widow of Francis Sheehy-Skeffington, and a republican and an outspoken feminist in her own right) and Countess Markievicz were imprisoned in Holloway Prison in London as a result of their republican activities. Patricia was a regular visitor to them. A letter from Countess Markievicz written from the prison states that 'We got some lovely marmalade – I think it must have been Patricia's.' It most probably was Patricia's, since she rated edible treats very highly, as we have seen! She also ordered a comfortable chair for the Countess, who was finding the hardships of Holloway difficult but would never bemoan her lot. It is a measure of the admiration which people felt for this brave woman that, when the London store in question discovered that the chair was intended for the Countess, they insisted on sending a much better-quality one – at no extra charge! Later, in appreciation, Patricia received from Countess Markievicz a smuggled picture of 'a green-clad soldier, pale and exhausted, supported by the queenly figure of Éire in a flowing cloak.'[4] This picture was to remain one of Patricia's most treasured possessions for the rest of her life.

Patricia Lynch's involvement with the nationalist cause was peripheral in that she was never in the front line of any military action and was never imprisoned. She always declared herself a nationalist, however, and her proudest moments were those spent in the company of, or providing support for, the brave women in the aftermath of 1916.

The Pankhursts' direct influence on the question of votes for women virtually ended with the war effort, but they had the great satisfaction of seeing the fruits of their campaign. On 30 January 1917, a Parliamentary Conference recommended giving the vote to married women of thirty years of age and over. On 28 December 1918, women, for the first time, cast their votes in a United Kingdom general election. Out of the 1,600 candidates, seventeen were women; the only successful female candidate was Countess Markievicz, who was elected to Westminster as a Sinn Féin MP. The Countess declared that it was against her principles to take the oath of allegiance to the king, and consequently she could not attend Parliament. Notwithstanding, her election was a triumph for the feminist movement.

The close involvement of Patricia Lynch with both feminism and nationalism make her a powerful icon of her age. All through her life, she remained deeply committed to the ideals of freedom and social justice. This is reflected in an appeal which she made in *An Phoblacht* on 19 March 1932 for public acknowledgement of Maud Gonne MacBride's efforts during the dark days at the birth of the new State:

> A Chara,
> Now that Ireland's political prisoners have been freed, may I suggest that national recognition should be made of the magnificent work of Madame Gonne MacBride for political prisoners, reaching back to treason felony days and the time of the Land League?[5]

There is no record of any response to this appeal.

Patricia's love of her native country extended to attempts to boost the flagging tourist industry by encouraging people to visit Ireland and not to be put off by reports, in the aftermath of the

Rising, of tanks and the sound of gunfire. On 23 July 1920, she wrote an article for the British *Daily Independent* in which she said:

> The sounds we hear are the sweeping of the rain-laden wind among the trees, the splashing of water falling over rocks into a pool, the lowing of cattle. The sights which greet our eyes are wonderful stretches of dark mountains, ruined cottages, low, white farm buildings and sudden glimpses of sunlit sea between equally sudden showers.[6]

'A real live hobby!' she said wonderingly.   [Page 22

8

GETTING STARTED

When World War I ended in November 1918, Patricia Lynch was an independent-minded young woman of twenty-four, with many contacts in the literary world and an unwavering commitment to her writing. She still had her mother, Nora, and her brother, Patrick Henry, but now her relationship with them had changed: she was no longer the vulnerable youngster who never knew where her next home would be. Patrick Henry was a successful, intelligent man who could speak Irish, French, German and a little Arabic, and his career in accountancy was flourishing. Money was no longer tight, and he could provide a comfortable home for his mother. He and Patricia were very loving siblings, as well as being good friends. They shared interests and often went to social events, plays, poetry readings, and political and nationalist rallies together. His friends were hers, and she, being the more outgoing of the two, introduced him to many of her associates. The large gap in their ages now seemed unimportant.

One thing had not changed from the earlier period, though, and that was the great closeness between Nora and her son, and the enormous sense of responsibility which Patrick Henry felt with regard to his mother's welfare. From the time when he was a young teenager, he had looked after her and had accompanied her on her quests; he had been her travelling companion, her confidant and her breadwinner. Now, in his thirties, Patrick Henry was still the most important person in her life. This was a heavy burden for any young man to carry, but he carried it lovingly. In one sense, the fact that he was prepared to continue in this role freed Patricia to follow her own star. Although she and Nora had a warm relationship, Patricia was not involved in her mother's life to the same extent as Patrick Henry was.

Patricia's career as a journalist was broadening. Her stint on the *Workers' Dreadnought* proved to be an excellent training ground, and it also gave her a foot on the ladder of magazine journalism. She started work for the *Christian Commonwealth,* a weekly general-interest magazine, for which she wrote advice columns, fashion items and news snippets. She also conducted interviews with well-known personalities – something at which she was particularly good, given her outgoing, friendly attitude. She had a knack of drawing people out and encouraging them to talk comfortably about themselves. Also, having secured her material, she very often became good friends with her subjects. As a writer, she was fluent and imaginative, and her interviews were always popular among the magazine's readers. One of her assignments was to interview the writer Edith Nesbit, who, as we have seen, had long been a role model for her.

To be in the position of conducting an interview with her idol was a humbling experience for Patricia. To prepare for the interview, she had re-read Nesbit's book *The Magic City.* When Patricia entered the old house called Well Hall in Kent, where Edith Nesbit, now an old lady, lived, Patricia remembers that: 'I felt as if the gates of that magic city had opened before me.'[1] As was often the case with Patricia, she herself made a deep impression on her subject, and from that time on Edith Nesbit took a personal interest in the fledgling writer. She sent Patricia home with an armful of flowers and a basket of apples from her garden, telling her that they were a little gift for her mother Nora.

Earning her living as a journalist in London was quite an achievement for Patricia. At that time, the majority of journalists – and almost all magazine editors – were men, so for Patricia to be given the chance to do interviews with celebrities reflected the high esteem in which she was held as a writer. She also contributed to what used to be called 'women's page' material. As well as being an important apprenticeship for her, it demonstrated her skills in connecting with her readers and relating to their problems. The years of writing letters to her mother and brother as they made their way around the world in search of Mr Blanchard's 'gold mine' were also undoubtedly an important part of the groundwork for her life as a writer. For now, life was good, and Patricia was enjoying London – as any young woman with an exciting job would have done. She had a stimulating social life, a challenging job, money of her own, good friends and, most important of all, her family around her. Then suddenly, everything changed.

Patrick Henry had been feeling a little off form for some time but, out of his usual concern for his mother, he had played down his illness and had done his best to carry on as normal. One night, after Nora had gone to bed, he had sat Patricia down with him and asked her to promise that, if anything were to happen to him, she would look after Nora and never leave her. Patricia, not thinking much about this, had of course promised to do so. She describes the events of the following day as follows:

> We were sitting side by side on the big, comfortable sofa. Suddenly his head seemed to become heavy and I looked at him in surprise. His eyes were closed, his face white, his lips pressed firmly together. 'Henry!' I cried. 'Henry Patrick [*sic*], are you ill?' My mother leaned forward and took his hand in hers. 'Henry,' she whispered. 'No. No. This can't be the end!' And then Henry Patrick died as quietly and unobtrusively as he had lived.[2]

It did not seem possible to Patricia that Patrick Henry, who had been father, brother, breadwinner and companion, should now be gone. Nora was inconsolable. Patricia felt inadequate to the task of dealing with both her own grief and with Nora's shocked withdrawal from her. She describes very movingly her mother's reaction to her son's death:

> There were only two of us now, where there had always been three. I couldn't get used to that, nor could my mother. It was worse for her. The third had been my brother. He was more than a son. There were only eighteen years between them and he was old for his age. She was very young until now. That night when he died she froze. Her eyes went blank, her face white. She never laughed again.

She goes on to say:

> For my mother it seemed the end of the world. For me it was unbelievable. He had been more like a father than a brother, and the two of us, my mother and I, were like two shipwrecked mariners.[3]

Patricia, who so many years before had learned how to detach herself from her own pain and loneliness, now had a far more difficult situation to cope with, in that she had become the sole support for her mother. Nora had married young, going straight from the care of her father into the care of her husband. Then, when Timothy Patrick took off for faraway places, she went back under the wing of Grandfather Lynch once more. When she was widowed, Patrick Henry had taken on the burden of caring for her. At no time was Nora obliged to stand alone, or to test her own resourcefulness. She had never worked, except for her lacemaking. She was never financially independent, and any money she had had she had used to travel, in a constant search for an elusive nirvana. Mrs Hennessy's description of her as being 'some sort of a changeling' was apt, in that she never conformed to the norm for a woman of her time. Now all her strength seemed to seep away: Patricia could see why her brother had made her promise that she would never leave her mother and would always look after her.

With Patrick Henry gone, the Lynches' financial situation once again became critical. In the long term, Patricia's earnings would not cover living expenses for the two of them, as well as the rent on their London home. So when a period of mourning had passed, Patricia had to give serious thought to what would be the best thing for Nora and her to do. Nora was little help when it came to Patricia making that decision, although she was amenable to going wherever Patricia might choose to bring her. Patricia knew that her mother would be happier in Ireland than in England, and so she set the wheels in motion for their return to Ireland.

Patricia's social life in London had always revolved around the societies of which she was a member and the causes she championed. These causes were many, from feminism to nationalism and workers' rights. Patrick Henry had shared her dedication to attempting to right the injustices which they both saw around them, and he had thrown his weight behind the various organisations that were in the forefront of the fight against social and political tyranny. One of his comrades in this battle was a young man called Richard Michael Fox, a fearless advocate of workers' rights, of better living conditions for the poor, of socialist principles and of self-government for the Irish people. Patricia had looked up to this man and had admired the stance which he had taken on the issues in which he believed. Although, in the early days of their friendship, Richard Fox would have viewed her as the younger sister who tagged on to her brother's friends, he was destined to become a pivotal figure in Patricia's future. At this early stage, they were friends drawn together by their ideals, but later their friendship was to develop into a deep respect and an enduring love. Richard M. Fox was to be Patricia's pillar of strength throughout a marriage that was to last for almost fifty years. He was the person who would at last give Patricia the security she craved, and which would free her to unleash her creative energies.

9

R. M. FOX

Richard Michael Fox was born in Leeds on 13 November 1891, the second of four sons, of parents who had vaguely Irish antecedents. The family, which Patricia referred to as being 'Anglo-Irish', moved to London before the birth of their fourth son, George, and, according to the 1901 Census, resided at Bruce Castle Road, Tottenham, London N17. Richard's father was a skilled engineering workman who was also a talented inventor. He worked for a company which manufactured and marketed automatic machines of the 'penny-in-the-slot' kind. This work prompted him to devise all sorts of new and commercially viable slot-machine games, based on horse racing, boxing, balloon racing and other things. He lacked the business sense to patent these games or to market them himself, however. Instead, he handed the rights to them over to his company, receiving a pittance in exchange. As a result, he would never become rich from his ideas, while his company made big profits from them.

He was also, like his son Richard, a champion of the rights of his co-workers, and made himself unpopular with his employers by always taking the side of the employees in company disputes. No matter how trivial the dispute might seem in the eyes of the company, if Fox felt that there was any injustice involved, he would take up the case. This, of course, did not go down well with his bosses, and it no doubt put a brake on his prospects of advancement up the company ladder. Years later, Patricia wrote of him as being 'a playboy, a problem to them and to himself, for he had great ambition but no talent.'[1]

R. M. Fox's mother had been a school headmistress. She was a great believer in education, and taught her sons to value the written word and to expand their minds through reading good literature. She was, in Patricia's words, 'a kind little woman'[2] who held the family together in thin times and encouraged her sons to be men of truth and integrity.

Richard was a voracious reader but was also a bit of a rebel, and this resulted in him leaving school in the autumn of 1905, before his fourteenth birthday, and striking out on his own to earn his living. From a very early age, he wanted to be a writer, but he also dreaded being a burden on his family. Not having the qualifications for anything else, he got a job in a factory, doing rough, unskilled work. He started work at six in the morning and worked solidly until six in the evening: it was a harsh, unrelenting existence for a young man. He could not afford public transport and so had to face an hour's walk each morning and evening. He joined the Socialist Party and later started attending night school. When he wasn't too exhausted, he wrote; his earliest writings dealt with his life in the factory. Many years later, in an article for the *Irish Digest* entitled 'Adventures of a Young Author', Fox relates how he wrote a series of imaginative sketches of industrial life, called 'Factory Echoes', which he hoped to have published in book form. The article tells its readers that he 'saw industry as a great monster squeezing the life out of myself and my fellows' and goes on to say that a possible escape route was offered to him when 'Miles Malleson, the actor and dramatist, was very encouraging, and gave me a letter to a publisher that he knew.'[3]

Although Malleson's kind offer would undoubtedly have opened doors for Fox and given him an opportunity to get away from the drudgery of his life, at this stage he had no opportunity to take it up. War had broken out, and young men were being conscripted for the army. Being a committed pacifist and a conscientious objector, Fox refused to join up. He denounced the conflict as an imperialist war and stated that no worker should volunteer to fight against his fellow workers of other countries.

He actively participated in anti-war marches and became a soapbox orator at Hyde Park Corner, highlighting the plight of the working classes. In fact, it was while he was orating on his soapbox in early 1916 that Patricia Lynch caught her first glimpse of the man who was to become such an important part of her life.

Fox also wrote political pamphlets voicing his antipathy to the exploitation of the masses by the few. One of these pamphlets, published in 1916, was called *The Rebel*. In it, Fox declares:

> We stand for working-class internationalism and economic freedom. We represent that growing force in modern society of an awakening working class. The men who own the land, factories etc. and the men who have to sell their energy to them stand as buyers and sellers in opposite camps.[4]

Such talk was dangerous in wartime England – and doubly dangerous when it came from a conscientious objector. Fox was arrested and spent almost three years in Wormwood Scrubs Prison. Here he continued to write political tracts, but he also wrote articles and tried his hand at poetry in an effort to assuage the harshness and loneliness of prison life. One such poem, dated February 1917, was entitled 'Night'. It begins:

> The shades of night are falling
> The soft cool breezes blow
> A sweet glad voice is calling
> The healing waters flow.

Fox wrote many more snippets of poetry in the same vein. They were all rather sentimental and not very original but were nonetheless an indication of the sensitivity of Fox's character, and evidence of the wrench it must have been for him to be incarcerated for almost three years in Wormwood Scrubs. For Patricia, this added to the aura of glamour surrounding him, and her admiration for him grew: not many young men of her acquaintance would have been prepared to give up those precious years for a deeply held belief.

When he was released from Wormwood Scrubs in April 1919, Fox took the letter which Miles Malleson, a well-known and respected actor, had given him three years earlier and presented it to the editor in question, with the vague explanation that he had been 'unavoidably delayed'! The editor was most impressed with this serious young man and agreed to read 'Factory Echoes'. The outcome was that he decided to publish the book, which created quite a stir and had moderate commercial success.

In 1914, shortly before the commencement of the war, Fox had been awarded a National Co-operative Scholarship to study at Ruskin College, Oxford, an independent college that specialised in providing educational opportunities for adults with few qualifications. The college claimed that its aim was 'to change the lives of those who need a second chance in education.' This too had to be put on hold, but now Fox returned to take up the scholarship and became a full-time student. He studied economics and political science and pursued extra-curricular studies in literature and psychology. On 13 July 1921, Richard Michael Fox from Ruskin College, Oxford, was awarded a Diploma in Economics and Political Science. He was now ready to begin his career as a political writer and journalist, and was also in a position to woo the sister of his best friend and colleague, Patrick Henry Lynch.

In the meantime, Patricia had returned to Ireland with her mother. Without Patrick Henry they both felt lost. Nora wanted to return to her roots, and Patricia, too, was anxious to live once more in Ireland. This time, they came not to Cork but to Dublin, where Patricia hoped there would be more work to be found. Their first task was to look for accommodation in a city which had been devastated by the Rising of 1916 and by the Civil War which followed. Patricia found rooms in a house in Leeson Street owned by a Mrs Laffens, but because the accommodation was on the top floor, and the stairs would be difficult for her mother, Patricia decided that it would not do. She could not possibly leave her mother there alone while she went out to work. She walked the streets in search of lodgings which they could afford, and where Nora could feel more settled. Finding nothing suitable, in desperation she finally put an advertisement in the *Evening Mail*. Following this enquiry, Patricia received a reply from a Mrs O'Dwyer, who seemed to have much more suitable accommodation to offer. Nora immediately warmed to this landlady, and Patricia, heartened by her response, kept quiet about the fact that the woman had ten children. 'My mother never seemed to me to care for children,' Patricia noted.[5] The whole family took to Nora, however: they were kind to her and regarded her as an honoured member of the household. This left Patricia free to search for work.

Louie Bennett, one of the women involved in the Rising and a close friend of Hannah Sheehy-Skeffington, found a job in an office for Patricia. Louie Bennett was also a friend and close associate of R. M. Fox.; in fact, many years later, Fox was to write her biography. This office work was not exactly what Patricia would have chosen – she was looking for journalistic work – but it brought in a wage and enabled her to keep a sharp lookout for something that was more in line with her interests. She was also producing articles and interviewing people of interest in the hope of being able to sell the pieces on a freelance basis.

Life was drab and lonely for Patricia. She describes this time for her as like being on a desert island; but for her mother's presence, she would have found it unbearable. She missed her brother, who had always been such a strong presence in the family. She also desperately missed R. M. Fox, for whom her feelings, in his absence, were growing even deeper. His letters to her were full of messages of love and affection, and whenever he got the chance, he came over to Dublin to visit her. Nora was very fond of 'R.M.', as she called him, and at one stage urged Patricia to marry him. 'But he hasn't asked me,' Patricia replied. 'No, but he will,' Nora assured her.[6] Nora's health was gradually deteriorating, and she wanted more than anything else to see her daughter settled with a good man who would look after her. Her own marriage, with her husband following his dreams to far-flung parts of the world, had never provided her with any kind of security. Although she would never hear a word against him, this was not what she wanted for her only daughter.

Nora died early in 1922. Patricia packed up their few belongings and moved out of the rented rooms. She was now truly alone in the world: there was no one left of her family, and she was unsure as to where her future lay. She moved back to London for a while, where R.M.'s mother befriended her, and urged her to marry 'Dick', as she called him. R.M. and Patricia were becoming even closer and more dependent on one another, and this time, while they were both in London, he did propose to her. Patricia accepted, and she says that 'it was one of the wisest and happiest decisions of my life.'[7]

Patricia and R.M. began to plot out their future together: they were both convinced that that future would lie in Ireland. They even thought of opening a bookshop together to supplement what they knew would be the meagre income they would earn from writing. At this stage, Patricia was in Dublin, while R.M. stayed on in London. In a letter dated 1 June 1922, R.M. asked Patricia: 'Have you written to the Vartry Road priest yet? And is the shop coming out of the mists into reality? I guess we'll want to start about the end of August won't we?' He goes on: 'We can help each other all the way, and that's what we're going to do.'[8] In another letter, dated 4 July 1922, he writes: 'Since I have loved you it has made all the difference to me. It makes things seem worthwhile now.'[9] It wasn't only Patricia who had found an anchor and a soulmate. R. M. Fox, to all intents and purposes a strong-minded, self-sufficient, independent individual, had fallen deeply in love with this unusual Irish girl and could not now imagine life without her at his side.

Patricia Nora Lynch and Richard Michael Fox were married in the Church of Saint Francis de Sales on High Road in Tottenham, Middlesex, on Wednesday 4 October 1922. The celebrant was Father George W. Dibben, and the marriage was subsequently registered by W. Grimaldi, Superintendent Registrar, White Hart Lane, Lower Tottenham. The bride was aged twenty-eight and the groom thirty-one. The couple's plan was to return to Ireland after the wedding and together carve out careers as writers. As Fox himself put it: 'We were going to write, to cultivate literature and its humbler companion, journalism – on a little oatmeal, if necessary.'[10]

10

MARRIED LIFE

The young married couple were well aware of the problems that lay ahead. Money would be tight, finding a suitable house could be difficult, and it would be hard to break into journalism in Ireland – and harder still to get any fiction published. Full of high spirits and completely confident that their mutual love would see them through, however, they decided that, before settling down to the business of earning a living, they would spend most of their savings on a continental tour. This was a brave and risky venture, but they desperately wanted to travel together and feared that it would become harder rather than easier to do this if they waited until their careers were established and they had found a niche in the market in Ireland. Besides, they wanted a honeymoon – and a truly memorable one, at that.

The first city they went to was Paris, where R.M. had friends, from his campaigning days, to whom he was anxious to introduce his young bride. From Paris they went to Brussels, where the King of Italy was being received with military honours, and from Brussels it was a short step to Bruges. Patricia was eager to show her new husband the city where she had spent so many months, and where she had felt so much at home with the Baerasaels. Memories crowded in on her. She rushed R.M. around from sight to sight, pointing out the little streets where she had shopped, the building where she had been so ill, lying feverishly in bed, listening to the bells, and the Grande Basin where she had skated during the big freeze. Her memories sometimes deceived her. Everything now seemed much smaller and far less dramatic. But R.M. was an appreciative audience, expressing wonder and interest in all that she pointed out, and entering into the spirit of Patricia's trip down memory lane.

Their next stop was Germany – and Berlin in particular, a city crippled by industrial and political unrest. The moral disintegration of the Weimar Republic, the plummeting mark and the economic crisis all combined to make Berlin a less than pleasant place for a liberal socialist like Fox to be. He was shocked by what he saw there, and by the awful atmosphere which permeated everyday life. He called Berlin 'a city of violent contrasts . . . where the people are resigned to their fate'.[1] The couple cut short their honeymoon after Berlin, and returned to Dublin as the Civil War was drawing to a bitter close.

Their first home together was in Rathfarnham, which was at that time out in the country. It was a spacious house with a large garden, which Patricia loved to cultivate, and the rent was five shillings a week, fully furnished! It was also within easy reach of the Dublin Mountains. The young couple spent many happy afternoons exploring the terrain, walking for miles along deserted pathways, braving wind and rain. In the evenings, they would light the fire and, invigorated by the air and the exercise, settle down to write. This was how they had determined their lives would be from now on, and they were resolved to succeed, even if they would have to exist on that mythical oatmeal. And indeed, for a long time it appeared that they would need to live very frugally, as the rejection slips piled up and article after article was returned to them.

In 1923, they left the rented house to move closer to the city – into a tall house in Glasnevin from whose upstairs windows they could still see their beloved Dublin Mountains. There they turned two rooms into individual studies, each with a large bookcase, a desk and a chair. R.M. joked that, although his bookcase was larger than his wife's, Patricia's was very soon more laden down with books than his. Like Grandfather Lynch, Patricia had an insatiable appetite for reading matter.

Eventually, R. M. Fox got the break which was to establish

him as a literary journalist. This came about through his meeting with that towering figure of the Irish literary renaissance, George Russell. Russell was the saviour of many a fledgling writer. A poet and mystic, Russell's own quasi-philosophical writing was not particularly influential, but he had a great influence on young writers. At one time or another, he was a mentor to James Joyce, Pádraic Colum, James Stephens, Frank O'Connor, Padraic Fallon, Austin Clarke and Patrick Kavanagh, among others. W. B. Yeats mockingly called these protégés 'Æ's Canaries'. Indeed, O'Connor remembers Russell as being 'The friend of every young writer. He read our manuscripts, printed us, found us publishers, supervised our reading. He even wanted to arrange our marriages.'[2]

Æ held open house at his home at 17 Rathgar Avenue on Sunday nights, and these soirées were an important source of literary contacts for aspiring writers. From 1905, Æ had edited the *Irish Homestead,* a magazine which promoted the idea of co-operativism. In 1923, he became editor of the *Irish Statesman,* which was to provide an outlet for liberal viewpoints and was also a platform for emerging creative writers, who found in Russell a sharp and sympathetic critic. He stressed the association between the writer and national aspirations but was horrified by the brutality and destructiveness of the Civil War. Like R. M. Fox, he abhorred the idea of mass industrialisation, which he felt dehumanised people. His aspirations for the new Ireland, following the Civil War, were for a nation which would not only draw on its own past for inspiration but also incorporate the best of other cultures. He wrote that 'we shall find much inspiration and beauty in our own past but we have to ransack world literature, world history, world science, and study our national contemporaries and graft what we learn into our own national traditions, if we are not to fade out of the list of civilised nations.'[3] His deep humanity and social conscience endeared him to Fox, who became a great admirer of his.

Having met and spoken to Fox, Æ agreed to let him review books for the *Irish Homestead* and later for the *Irish Statesman.* His reviews in the *Irish Statesman* in particular brought Fox's name to public attention. He then wrote an article on the death of Lenin, and submitted it to Russell. Æ accepted the article, although, fearing that an article on Lenin would prove to be contentious, he wryly remarked that 'I shall get into trouble for this, but I will publish it.'[4]

When Fox produced a book on industrial problems, entitled *The Iron Visions*, Æ generously wrote a foreword to it, in which he said that 'I like my friend Mr Fox's book because he has known for himself and of others how deadening to human life the vast mechanisms of modern industry may be.'[5] Many years later, in 1944, Fox wrote a tribute to Æ, who had died in 1935, in the magazine *Progress Monthly*. He was generous in his praise of the great man and of his achievements. Fox wrote of Æ:

> Not only did he serve progressive and humanitarian ends in the great labour struggle, but he was one of the pioneers with Yeats in the Literary Renaissance in Ireland known as the Celtic Twilight because of its mist-laden beauty.[6]

And so, thanks to the break George Russell had given him, and to the many contacts in the literary world that he had made through Russell, the name 'R. M. Fox' became known to the readers of liberal magazines, labour journals and daily newspapers. Gradually, Fox also became an astute theatre critic and a well-known face at opening nights at the Abbey Theatre. Talent and hard work were of course part of the equation, but there is no doubt that Æ's influence was the key which opened the door for him.

Meanwhile, in the other study in the big house at 39 The Rise, Glasnevin, Patricia was beavering away at her writing. Keeping food on the table, and staying on top of living expenses, meant that most of her creative energies were spent on writing articles for various magazines. She was also writing short stories, however, and doing the spadework for the creation of those tales of Irish folklore and imagination which would later become her forte. Very often, magazines which published Fox's socialist articles also accepted short stories from Patricia. One such in those early days was the *Co-operative News,* which published a whimsical, tear-jerking story of Patricia's called 'The Organ Grinder' in its issue of 24 February 1923.

She managed to have her early stories published in magazines in the UK also, writing a touching little story called 'The Girl Who Hated Christmas' for *Family Herald* (a magazine priced at twopence) in their issue of 24 December 1927. She also wrote for *Strand* magazine, where many years ago earlier she had read and been so impressed by the stories of Edith Nesbit, with their tantalising mixture of fantasy and reality. In fact, Patricia kept beside her desk an interview which Nesbit had given in the *Christian Commonwealth,* dated 27 February 1918, in which Nesbit stated:

> I love children, but books for children cannot be written by those who merely like or study them. It is only possible for those who remember what one felt like as a child, and have never quite grown away from it.

Patricia had underlined this statement. She had also underlined the following from the same interview:

> We want more imagination. When the Kaiser wanted to establish militarism he forbade fairy tales, folk tales, songs, games and dances in the schools, and ordered drill instead. That is the worst thing he has done. We forget that ideas and individuality can be killed as well as human beings.[7]

Patricia Lynch was clearly greatly impressed by these statements. Her own childhood had been traumatic in many ways, but it had also given her a powerful insight into the pains, fears and joys of being a child, and she could sympathise with all that children felt and suffered. Her imagination was highly tuned, and folklore and myth were a rich part of the shaping of that imagination. She resolved to put on paper the sort of material which she herself had found so enriching, thereby to enrich the childhoods of countless other children.

PART TWO

11

The Writer Is Born

Patricia, settled into domestic life with R.M. by her side and happier than she had ever remembered being before, now devoted all her time and energies to her writing. 'To be living in Ireland', she wrote, 'earning my living at writing, to be married to someone who looked at Ireland with the same vision as my own, that was happiness!'[1] It was a time of extraordinary productivity for the two writers. R.M., through his introductions from George Russell, soon found himself in demand as a freelance journalist and drama critic. A letter dated September 1929 from Æ, who at this time was editor of the *Irish Statesman,* incorporating the *Irish Homestead,* shows the kindness and big-heartedness of this great character. 'My dear Fox', he writes, 'I am sure you would make an admirable editor in the *Co-operative Journal.'*

In a fairly short space of time, Fox became sub-editor of the *Irish Press,* drama critic for the *Evening Mail* and Dublin correspondent with the *Manchester Guardian.* He was also theatre critic for the *Evening Herald* and the *Irish Press,* and a prolific writer of articles and political tracts. His larger works included *Rebel Irishwomen* (1935), *The Story of the Irish Struggle* (1938), *Smokey Crusade* (1938), *The History of the Irish Citizen Army* (1943) and biographies of James Connolly, Jim Larkin and Louie Bennett.

As they became established in Dublin, he and Patricia moved in circles of people involved in the politics of labour, mingling with Seán O'Casey, Peadar O'Donnell, Liam O'Flaherty, Erskine Childers and others. They also held an 'open house' once a week at their home, providing a venue for other writers and artists to gather, talk and exchange ideas.

Patricia, too, was forging ahead with her writing. Her first published book was *The Green Dragon,* released in 1925 by George Harrap & Co. of London and illustrated by Dorothy Hardy. This book had a short print run, but it was important in that it gave Patricia the confidence to tackle the longer narrative form. In 1931, she wrote *The Cobbler's Apprentice,* which was published by The Talbot Press in time to win a national literary award at the Tailteann Festival in Dublin in 1932. This story relates the plight of a young boy who is taken out of his rural background and sent to the nearby town to be apprenticed to a cobbler. The cobbler is a cold and severe master, and the boy's isolation and loneliness are overwhelming, until he discovers the companionship of the domestic cat and dog, with whom he finds he is able to communicate in animal language. This was the first of many of Patricia Lynch's stories where lonely or deprived children discover the facility of understanding animal language. The crossover in this story from the animal world to the child's world is made so smoothly that it seems perfectly reasonable to the reader. Patricia herself declared:

> My only aim was to tell a story that would hold my audience. How far one can separate the intertwined worlds of fact and fantasy is difficult to say. And whether they should be separated is more difficult still.[2]

The judges for the Tailteann Literary Award – an award which was set up to encourage native writers – were in agreement that Patricia had got the mixture of fact and fantasy exactly right with *The Cobbler's Apprentice* and were generous in their praise for the book. Their comments, dated 17 November 1931 and signed by C. Gifford Wilson, make for interesting reading. They report on the book as follows:

1   A delightful story on the old lines, appealing and amusing. A work of distinction. Marks: 80 percent.

2   This is a fairy story true to the old tradition and all
the better for that. Shamus the Cobbler's Apprentice is
considered to be a little weak in the head, but he has a
good heart which serves him in good stead through
many adventures with a Wise Woman and a Changeling
and a Leprachaun [*sic*] and other interesting characters.
Marks: 70 percent.[3]

To be awarded this prize and to be officially recognised as a
culturally important writer for children in the Ireland of the
1930s was a great honour for Patricia and served as an important
spur to her writing career. Whether the award was of any great
financial significance, however, was open to question: there was
probably very little cash involved.

Patricia's first big breakthrough came when she submitted
three children's stories to the *Irish Press* – where R.M. was a sub-
editor. The editor saw these stories as part of a sequence and
agreed to accept them as a serial. Patricia was taken aback, since
she had never envisaged them as anything other than individual
short stories. She was not going to let this chance slip through
her fingers, however. The serial was published, under the title
'The Turf-Cutter's Children', with beautiful illustrations by
George Altendorf, who had been assistant art editor of the *Irish
Press* since 1929. Altendorf, whose father was from Dresden and
whose brother was one of the artists in the Harry Clarke Studios,
had attended the Dublin Metropolitan School of Art and was a
pupil of the distinguished Seán Keating. (Altendorf announced
in his diary that 'Mr Keating says my stuff is very good! EURE-
KA!')[4]

The serial was hugely popular with the readers. It ran for
three years, and by the time it had finished Patricia had, as she
says herself, enough material for three books: *The Turf-Cutter's
Donkey, The Turf-Cutter's Donkey Goes Visiting* and *The Turf-Cutter's
Donkey Kicks Up His Heels.*

The Turf-Cutter's Donkey, published by Dent & Sons of London in 1934, is considered to be a children's classic and is probably the best-known and most widely read of all Lynch's books. The book features the convincingly drawn children Seamus and Eileen and a loveable little grey donkey called Long Ears. It is described by the author on the flyleaf as 'an Irish Story of Mystery and Adventure' and is dedicated 'To Nora and Patrick: My Companions in Tir Na N-Og'. In it, she draws heavily on ancient legends of the Tuatha Dé Danann, who are said to have inhabited Ireland during the Bronze Age.

The children enter a magical world, where they meet characters from Ireland's legendary past. The brave little donkey – who has a personality uniquely his own, and whose conversations with the young protagonists seem completely natural – accompanies them on all kinds of adventures. Seamus and Eileen travel through time and through history but eventually arrive back home safely. The security of their cabin, with its welcoming fire, is the ultimate reward at the end of their dangerous travels:

> They could see the whitewashed cabin at the edge of the
> bog, and the blue turf-smoke rising from the chimney. In
> all the wonderful past they had not seen anything more
> lovely.[5]

The narrator ends the story on this appealing note, as the children leave their world of fantasy and legend, and reconnect with reality. This was a book – exciting, fast-moving and colourful – to stretch the imagination of any child. It was a story in which Lynch gathered together all the things she liked about Ireland – the donkeys, the turf, the children, the legends – and wove them together seamlessly.

Dent commissioned Jack B. Yeats to illustrate the book, and his wonderful line drawings perfectly capture the mood of the narrative. Patricia liked Yeats's interpretations best of all her many famous illustrators because she felt that they were entirely in the spirit of the book. Yeats captured the magic of the world which Patricia had created, and this sense of romance and mystery are reflected in the lines of his drawings.

Jack Yeats, the brother of the poet W. B. Yeats and son of the portrait painter John Butler Yeats, was himself very much part of the Irish cultural renaissance. His work in many ways parallels in visual art what his brother was doing in literature, in that both tried to preserve the folklore and myths of an imagined heroic past. In 1911, he illustrated a volume of J. M. Synge's essays with illustrations worthy of Synge's exuberant writing style. Yeats's early watercolours were representations of Irish landscapes and peasant people, though his later work became much more impressionistic. He was also a superb black-and-white illustrator: he contributed to *Punch* magazine for more than thirty years, using the name 'W. Bird'. The flowing lines of his drawings in *The Turf-Cutter's Donkey* are ample evidence of this skill. It was during his middle period as an artist that he took on the commission to illustrate Patricia Lynch's book: the tale of fantasy and folklore clearly appealed to his artistic imagination. As he had written to W.B., Jack Yeats believed that 'By logic and reason we die hourly, by imagination we live.'[6]

It seems likely that Patricia herself approached the great man to ask him if he would be willing to provide the illustrations for her book. A letter dated 15 May 1934 from 18 Fitzwilliam Square, Dublin, goes as follows:

Dear Madame,

Thank you for your letter of May 13 and for your book *The Cobbler's Apprentice,* which came today. This is a fine and pleasant book. I saw your story 'The Turf-Cutter's Children' coming out in the *Irish Press,* but the instalments were too tiring to read with comfort. I am sure it is a good book. I am writing to Messrs Dent now.

Jack B. Yeats[7]

In 1935, Dent and Sons were ready to publish the latest tale of Eileen, Seamus and Long Ears. This was called *The Turf-Cutter's*

Donkey Goes Visiting: The Story of an Island Holiday and was dedicated to R. M. Fox. The book was again a tale of adventure and fantasy, with everyday events shifting into the mythical world of Tír na nÓg. The children follow a mountain path to enter a world of legend and myth. Two changelings take their place in the real world, and Seamus and Eileen are tempted to remain in Tír na nÓg. Eventually, however, they find their way back home, led by Long Ears, and once again there is nothing more wonderful than this homecoming, with the security of the cabin, the fire blazing and the kettle singing by the hearth, and a hot smell of potato cake wafting out to greet them. As is ever the case for Lynch's protagonists, happiness is having a home to return to.

With the book ready for publication, Patricia wrote again to Jack Yeats to ask him if he would do the illustrations. Yeats was not too happy with his previous treatment by the publishers Dent and Sons, however. On 21 June 1935, he wrote to Patricia:

> Dear Miss Lynch,
>
> Thank you for your letter of yesterday. I am sure I would enjoy illustrating your new book *The Turf-Cutter's Donkey Goes Visiting,* as I did the first book. I am now writing to Dent to take the matter up with them again, but their payment to me for the first book was not enough.
>
> I am, yours sincerely,
> Jack B. Yeats.

Obviously Dent were not prepared to increase the payment: in another letter to Lynch, dated 26 June 1935, Yeats writes that Dent were 'unable to accept the offer I made for the illustrating of your book'. A further letter followed on 15 July:

> Dear Miss Lynch,
>
> I am sorry for the bother about your book. I would suggest that you try another publisher – of a more generous kind than Dent. You could assure them that Dent was willing to publish your book but the trouble was my

terms – £100 on handing over the illustrations, the originals of course to be returned to me.

I am, yours sincerely,

Jack B. Yeats[8]

Given the choice between her publisher and her illustrator, Patricia opted to stick with Dent. The book was published later that year, with illustrations by George Altendorf, who had produced the drawings for the serial in the *Irish Press*. The attention to detail and use of rich colour make Altendorf's illustrations a worthy follow-up to the Yeats illustrations in her previous book, and they capture the mood of the book very successfully.

The Turf-Cutter's Donkey and *The Turf-Cutter's Donkey Goes Visiting* were so popular that they were immediately taken up by the American publishers E. P. Dutton & Co. of New York, who published them in 1935 and 1936 respectively. The third book in the trilogy, *The Turf-Cutter's Donkey Kicks Up His Heels*, was published by Dutton in 1939, before its publication by Dent. This change in the usual order of publication was because of some confusion in the publishing contracts. A letter to Patricia from Dutton & Co. dated 27 October 1938 stated that 'We have a contract with you for the publication of *The Turf-Cutter's Donkey Kicks Up His Heels*, dated October 20 1937. Through misunderstanding it would appear that this contract is in conflict with a contract you have with J. M. Dent and Sons.'[9] The misunderstanding was settled amicably, and Dutton continued to be the American publisher of subsequent books by Patricia Lynch.

The 1930s was an extremely productive era for Patricia. She quickly followed up on the success of the 'Turf-Cutter's Donkey' trilogy with two acclaimed books, *King of the Tinkers*, published in 1938, and the hugely successful *The Grey Goose of Kilnevin*, published in 1939.

King of the Tinkers was dedicated to 'the other Nora',

presumably Patricia's mother. It features the adventures of Miheal, who sets out for the 'Hiring Fair', is waylaid by a band of tinkers, and befriends a little tinker girl called Nora. The hiring fair was a feature of Irish rural society of the 1920s and 1930s. To modern readers, the practice of having young boys and girls parade in front of prospective employers in the hope of being hired as servant girls or farm labourers seems nothing short of barbaric. This was, however, a time of great economic hardship in Ireland, and rural children had to leave home early and search for employment as maids and labourers in the homes of better-off farmers. Life was often harsh for these youngsters, who were frequently made to work far beyond their physical capacity and for little reward. For many of them, it was a stopgap before taking the boat to England, where they gladly exchanged the drudgery of rural life for the lights and companionship of the cities. But to find an employer at the hiring fair was a priority, and young people went to great lengths to be hired at the fairs.

Patricia describes how the protagonist, Miheal, arrives at the line-up with his bundle, wearing his fine, heavy coat and looking his best. 'It would surely help him to get a good master,' he thinks as he joins the line-up. The other youths seem bigger and more worldly-wise than Miheal, and they jostle him and push him to the back of the line in order to have the advantage over him when the farmers come to view them. One boy warns him that 'The only master ye'll get when ye're new is one ye'll run away from before ye've been with him a week.' He goes on to tell Miheal that 'The last farm I went to I had to get up at five, milk six cows, light the fire, bring the turf and the water before I had a bite to eat. When I wasn't cleaning out the sties, I was stacking the turf, and when I wasn't stackin I was cuttin. 'Twas a terrible hard life.'[10] Miheal, however, was ready for hard work and poor living conditions – reflecting the low expectations of the time.

The story takes Miheal on many different and wondrous paths, with the magical Red Lanty, whom he meets along the road and who becomes his good friend, and with the tinker tribe and Yellow Handkerchief, the King of the Tinkers, before he finally ends up back at home with his widowed mother, where, as always, the cheerful fire and tea and barmbrack await him. Work and cruel employers will have to wait for another day!

The illustrations by Katharine C. Lloyd are strong and highly romanticised, but Patricia herself had some reservations about them. She wrote to her publishers, Dent and Sons, on 3 November 1947 to the effect that she was 'very disappointed in the illustrations for that book. . . . They weren't good at all.' She asked if it was possible to replace the jacket illustration – which was of the tinker chief, a very aggressive and sinister-looking character placed against a wooded background – with a picture of 'the old king in the caravan'.[11] This illustration was a much gentler one, showing an elderly bearded man driving a grey donkey which is pulling a tiny green caravan. Patricia obviously felt that the original cover was far too strong for her young audience and was anxious to tone down its impact. She was always very forthright about the way she wanted her books presented to the public: in none of her books does she confront the darker side of life. This point is made very strongly by Tom Mullins, a lecturer in the Education Department of University College Cork, in his unpublished lecture entitled 'The Eye of Innocence':

> There are rogues and tricksters present in her world, but that is all they ever are – rarely posing a serious threat to the republic of childhood. Being a romantic herself, perhaps that was a compromise she wanted to make – to stress the wonder and excitement of the world rather than anything else . . . who would want to give anything else to one's children?[12]

King of the Tinkers was the only one of Patricia's books to be illustrated by Katharine C. Lloyd – suggesting that what Patricia wanted, Patricia got. She was by now such a hot property with her publishers that they sat up and took note when she spoke her mind. In early October 1938, Eason's of Dublin had a window display featuring *King of the Tinkers,* and on 13 October Patricia herself made an appearance there to meet her public and auto-graph her book. This gave her great pleasure: she loved to meet her reading audience, especially the children, with whom she had a natural rapport.

With her next book, Patricia's popularity grew even stronger. Of all her books, *The Grey Goose of Kilnevin,* published in 1939, per-haps lingers longest in the minds of its readers. The book first appeared as a story in the *Irish Press,* with illustrations by George Altendorf, and was such a hit with its readers nationwide that Patricia submitted it to Dent and Sons in the form of a novel. The Irish artist Seán Keating, who had been art tutor to George Altendorf at the Metropolitan School of Art, was commissioned to supply the illustrations. Keating, a pupil of William Orpen and the foremost defender of traditional painting in Ireland at the time, visited the Aran Islands around 1913. Like Synge, he was one of those involved in creating the new artistic national con-sciousness which had been inspired by the Literary Renaissance. Keating was primarily a figurative painter, and his subjects were frequently men involved in the national struggle. The men in his illustrations in *The Grey Goose of Kilnevin* are larger-than-life figures, suggesting strength and reliability, while the women are sturdy, honest-looking countrywomen, in line with Patricia's own vision of rural Ireland. There is a sense of realism in these draw-ings which contrasts with the more mystical quality of the Jack Yeats illustrations.

The Grey Goose of Kilnevin is a magical and heart-warming, but completely unsentimental, story of a little girl's quest for love and acceptance. The little girl, Sheila, is the kitchen drudge for Fat Maggie, a loud, quarrelsome and very demanding mistress. Sheila meets up with the little grey goose, Betsy, who herself is ostracised by the rest of the flock because she is so small and plain, and who in her loneliness wanders away from the flock, conscious of the fact that she will never be able to measure up. Sheila and Betsy, both outcasts, strike up a friendship and a

Patricia, age six
(Reproduced with permission of the Trustees of
the National Library of Ireland)

ricia Lynch, age two and a half, with
favourite rag doll, Poosie
produced with permission of the Trustees
he National Library of Ireland)

The steeple of Shandon Church from the River Lee, from an oil
painting by Bridget O'Connell

View of Sunday's Well, Cork, with Daly's Bridge at right, early 1900s
Patricia Lynch was born in Sunday's Well on 4 June 1894
(Reproduced by permission of the Cork Public Museum)

'Eithne watched the gulls drifting
over the ship' by Isobel Morton-Sale,
from *Fiddler's Quest*

'It had started life by being a cabin'
by George Altendorf, from
The Turf-Cutter's Donkey Goes Visiting

IT HAD STARTED LIFE BY BEING A CABIN

[T]o leprechauns dragging toadstools
[ca]me marching by' by Eileen Coghlan,
[fro]m *Strangers at the Fair*

Two leprechauns, dragging toadstools, came marching in.

Studio portrait of Countess Markievicz at
Lissadell House in 1904, shortly before
she embraced the nationalist cause
(Reproduced with permission of the Trustees
of the National Library of Ireland)

THERE WERE THE LIGHTS OF HOME SHINING THROUGH THE DARKNESS

'There were the lights of home shining through the darkness' by Jack B. Yeats, from *Th
Turf-Cutter's Donkey*
(Reproduced by permission of the Estate of Jack B. Yeats)

R. M. Fox, circa 1950

Sean Keating's illustration for
flyleaf of *The Grey Goose of
Kilnevin*
(Reproduced by permission of t
Estate of Sean Keating)

Illustration for *Tinker Boy*
by Harry Kernoff RHA

'YE'RE A GRAN LITTLE DANCER, SO Y'ARE'

're a gran little dancer, so y'are' by Katherine C. Lloyd, from *King of the Tinkers*

Illustration by Elizabeth Rivers for
Grania of Castle O'Hara

Lynch with Eugene Lambert and the puppet Brogeen the leprechaun, used in the RTÉ
TV series *Brogeen Follows the Magic Tune,* based on the book of the same name by Lynch,
March 1969
(Reproduced by permission of the RTÉ Stills Library)

A view of puppets from *Brogeen Follows the Magic Tune* during studio filming in March 19
The puppets were made by Eugene and Mal Lambert of the Lambert Puppet Theatre,
the stories were adapted for television by Frank Kelly.
(Reproduced by permission of the RTÉ Stills Library)

partnership. Communication between the two is effortless, as in many of Lynch's other stories featuring children and animals, and together they become a team, brave enough to tackle the world. Their adventures are varied and exciting, entering into the realms of mythology and folk history, then drifting back to the harsh reality of a cruel world where the weak are vulnerable and those who are different are shunned. The language of the story is outstandingly beautiful, and in no sense modified for its young audience. Sheila and Betsy meet up with the Children of Lir, who are exiled from their home 'where the silver path meets the gold, and light and darkness are one', and Sheila tries to help them. She relates to Betsy the origins of these strange swan children, and Betsy responds to the prospect of a story with delighted anticipation:

> 'Once upon a time,' began Sheila, and the grey goose waggled her tail and hissed with pleasure, for she knew that this was the proper way to tell a story.[13]

The reader is drawn into this world, where anything is possible – a surreal world with its own rules and precepts, where people and animals journey together, and where the quest ultimately concludes with a return to the safe haven of home:

> 'We're really safe home now, Betsy,' says Sheila, and the apple woman affirms her delight in this homecoming with a whispered 'To be in a real house, wid real people, an not to be on the move – isn't that grand.'[14]

The Grey Goose of Kilnevin was a huge success for Patricia. When it was published in the United States, it was chosen by the Canon Hayes Literature Committee as one of the hundred best books, adult or juvenile, to be published in America in 1941. It was translated into many languages and reprinted in paperback form, and it remains to this day one of those books which, read as a child, stays in the adult memory. David Norris, senator and Joyce scholar, remembers the delight he got from his first reading of *The Grey Goose of Kilnevin* as a child, how he relished the 'interpenetration of the magic and the real world' and loved 'the porky grey goose, who sat and looked sideways at you.' Roy Foster, Carroll Professor of Irish History at Oxford University, voices the opinion of many when he says that '*The Grey Goose of Kilnevin* . . . is a book which I found, and still find, magic. I first read it when I was about six or seven, and when I read it to my own children they were transfixed by it. It conjures up a wonderful atmosphere of rural Ireland in an age of innocence, in the days of wandering ballad singers.'[15]

'For me,' Patricia Lynch wrote many years later, 'the most important ingredient in a child's book is the quality of imagination, that is of imaginative integrity.'[16] In *The Grey Goose of Kilnevin*, she certainly captured that quality in abundance. In this narrative also, with its poignant images, evocative language and assured style, there is evidence that she was gaining maturity and confidence as a writer.

12

LIFE IN THE 1940s

By the beginning of the 1940s, both Patricia and R.M. were well established in their careers and were part of the vibrant social life of Dublin's cultural circle. R.M. was closely involved with the theatre; as a respected drama critic, he was in contact with most of the stage personalities of the time. With the Abbey going from strength to strength and the Gate providing an important alternative, Dublin of the 1940s was a very theatre-conscious city. Personalities such as F. J. McCormick, Mícheál Mac Liammóir, Lord and Lady Longford, Siobhán McKenna, Cyril Cusack, were public figures, subjects of discussion, criticism and gossip, whose work and activities gave rise to much interest. Fox's profiles and critiques had an avid reading audience. Though his workload was prodigious, encompassing political tracts, theatre reviews, travel articles and biographies of well-known figures, R.M. still found time to assist Patricia in her work. He typed all her stories – stories which she handwrote in her neat, rather childish handwriting – and kept an eye on her business affairs and tax returns. Patricia, though shrewd enough about financial matters, was happy to leave all these things to her husband, freeing her to concentrate on her creative work.

In August 1940, the BBC accepted a script of *King of the Tinkers* for broadcast; the first part of this series went on air in *Children's Hour,* a popular radio programme for young listeners, that month. The series was broadcast in six parts, with Jim McDowell, Nan McGuigan, Harry S. Gibson (as the Tinker

Chief), James Stewart and John McMahon in the principal parts. The 'Turf-Cutter' series had been translated into several languages, and Patricia was also writing short stories for magazines such as *Strand, Garda Review* and *Good Housekeeping,* as well as writing radio articles, children's plays and articles for journals.

In 1941, Dent and Sons published *Fiddler's Quest,* and this was subsequently issued by Lynch's New York publishers in 1943. *Fiddler's Quest* was quite a departure for Patricia. The 1940s were frugal, depressed years in Britain, with the horrors of war casting a sombre shadow over the childhoods of British children. Irish children too suffered, in a society that was repressive, censorious and economically depressed and which was still embroiled in the bitterness provoked by the Civil War.

There were two ways for a children's writer to counter this gloom. The first was to produce a narrative where fairy tale and fantasy could lift the young reader above the everyday and into the realm of the magical. Patricia would have excelled at this, as she had done in so many of her narratives. The other was to engage the child in a story firmly based in reality and the everyday, and let the child identify with fictional characters whose lives were not too far removed from his or her own life. In the case of *Fiddler's Quest,* Patricia Lynch chose this latter course. Moreover, *Fiddler's Quest* differed from all the previous work she had produced in that it was the only book of hers which dealt directly with the political situation in Ireland.

This book was aimed at a slightly older readership than her other stories, and she dedicated it to her grandfather, the old Fenian member and classical scholar Tighe Lynch. He would have relished this story, dealing as it does with the political struggle in Ireland. Patricia must have had qualms about presenting the manuscript to her British publishers, but she need not have worried. Controversial as it may have seemed, they were more than happy to publish it. It is the story of Eithne Cadogan, the fiddler of the title, who comes to Ireland from her home in England to search for Inishcoppal, her ancestral home, and for her grandfather, the legendary 'King' Cadogan. The setting is urban – unusually for Patricia's work – and a great part of the action takes place in a Dublin devastated by the aftermath of the 1916 Rising and the Civil War. In some ways, the narrative exploits the romantic side of Irish nationalism. The hero, Nial Desmond, is a republican on the run from British soldiers, and Eithne and her friends, the Raffertys, are unwittingly caught up in political events, finding themselves in effect gun-running for 'the boys'. As an avowed nationalist, Lynch had no difficulty in creating an utterly believable backdrop to Eithne's adventures; given the author's own fractured childhood, Eithne's quest for a home and family, and her strong desire to belong, is convincingly portrayed. Early on in the narrative, we are told of Eithne's loneliness, and about how tired she is of always going to strange places.

The narrative in *Fiddler's Quest* is gripping enough to hold the attention of older children, the characters are lively and convincing, and the setting is a wonderful journey into Dublin city and environs at the time of 'the Troubles'. There are no talking animals, and no fantasy world, but instead a world where family life is strong and where people pull together and share the good times and the bad in equal measure. Ethne and the young Raffertys join the throng heading for Dublin's Moore Street on a Saturday evening to pick up the best value in fruit and vegetables. ''Tis there the better part of Dublin goes marketing' explains Mrs Rafferty to Eithne, who is not familiar with this traditional Dublin street. 'And if ye wait till Saturday night, God alone knows the bargains ye'll get.'[1] They head up along the North Wall, past the small houses and the warehouses on the quays:

The wind had dropped and the Liffey was red with the sunset. Beyond O'Connell Bridge where the dome of the Four Courts and the spires of Christ Church and St Patrick's rose into the sky, clouds like great galleons had gathered. The lamps were glittering along the quays, but the cranes were still and only a few men idled in the shelter of the sheds.[2]

The narrative is full of music and colour, and the author's love of her adopted city is evident throughout. The culmination of Eithne's adventures is the appearance of her grandfather King Cadogan, and their return together to the mysterious island of Inishcoppal. This was a story with which children everywhere could identify, and one which conformed to Dent and Sons' later request to Patricia to 'keep your names of the child characters as simple as you can, and not too tongue-twistingly Irish'.[3]

The artist chosen to illustrate *Fiddler's Quest* was Isobel Morton-Sale. Her illustrations are vivid and fluid, befitting the fast-moving action of the narrative, with very lifelike characterisations. Morton-Sale was an experienced artist who was in great demand as an illustrator of children's books. She lived in Chelsea, had studied at the Central School of Art, and married a fellow student and artist, John Morton-Sale. Following their marriage, they moved to Dartmoor, where, like Patricia Lynch and R. M. Fox, they worked together in separate studios. After the war, they set up the Parnassus Gallery in London. This most English of artists may seem to have been an unusual choice for illustrating a children's book with such an Irish setting, but in fact the book had such a universal appeal, and the theme appealed to so many children in wartime England, that her illustrative skill proved to be an extra selling point. Today her work fetches huge prices at art auctions.

Even as *Fiddler's Quest* was being hailed as a new style of Patricia Lynch book, the author herself was hard at work on another story, which she called *Long Ears: The Story of a Little Grey Donkey*. This book, which was published by Dent and Sons in 1943, tells the tale of the strange adventures of a little donkey whose curiosity about the world outside his stable in Sky Farm is too tempting to resist. Long Ears, who has a wanderlust similar to that of so many of Lynch's protagonists, gets himself mixed up with cruel masters, tinker bands, magic roads and odd characters. He has a trusting nature and makes friends everywhere he goes; this leads him into some dark and dangerous situations, not least of which is when he is captured by the tinker chief and treated cruelly. This is familiar Patricia Lynch territory: a universe where animals speak, folklore intermingles with reality, and nature plays a dominant role.

With its impish and amusing illustrations by the artist Joan Kiddell-Monroe (who wrote to Patricia on 2 September 1943 that 'I was delighted to know you were so pleased with my illustrations. The charm of your stories makes it such a pleasure to illustrate them')[4], *Long Ears* became a universal favourite. Its popularity is attested to in a letter which Patricia received from the Dutch publishers L. J. Veen's Uitgeversmaatschappij N.V.:

> One of our acquaintances, Mrs. L. H. Moraux, who was in Ireland for the summer, gave us your book *Long Ears* to read, which we did with very much pleasure indeed. It gladdens the heart of a publisher to read a book for children improving but not tiring, nice with tension to make it a joy for children and grownups to read.

The writer, Mrs M. Th. Veen, goes on to say that 'we should very much like to acquire the Dutch translation rights to one of your other books, as *Long Ears* is already in hands.'[5]

Long Ears, with its great appeal to adults as well as youngsters, was an ideal book for reading aloud to children and had no difficulty crossing international boundaries. Along with *The Grey Goose of Kilnevin,* it was taken up by Penguin Books, which brought it out as a Puffin paperback in 1954.

These 'animal' stories, apart from the pleasure they gave their readers, could also be said to have focused public attention on the Irish attitude to animals. Donkeys bearing the brunt of mankind's cruelty has not been unique to Ireland, of course. Amongst those whose sensitivities were offended by the neglect of this 'beast of burden' was the poet Samuel Taylor Coleridge, who wrote:

> Poor little foal of an oppressed Race!
> I love the languid Patience of thy face:
> And oft with gentle hand I give thee bread,
> And clap thy rugged Coat, and pat thy head.[6]

Nonetheless, it is a sad fact that, as a nation, the Irish, particularly in previous generations, had quite a callous attitude towards animals. As J. M. Synge pointed out in relation to the inhabitants of the Aran Islands around the turn of the twentieth century:

> Although these people are kindly towards each other and to their children, they have no feeling for the sufferings of animals. . . . If two dogs fight at the slip when we are waiting for the steamer, the men are delighted and do all they can to keep up the fury of the battle. . . . They tie down donkeys' heads to their hoofs to keep them from straying, in a way that must cause horrible pain, and sometimes when I go into a cottage I find all the women of the place down on their knees plucking the feathers from live ducks and geese.'[7]

Synge was not the only writer to record the Irish peasants' callous attitude to animals. In *The Silver Fox,* Edith Somerville and Martin Ross noted that:

> The Irish peasant regards the sorrow for a mere animal as a childishness that is almost sinful, a tempting of ill fate in its parody of the grief rightly due only to what is described as 'a Christhian' [*sic*].[8]

Patricia Lynch's much-loved novel *The Turf-Cutter's Donkey* stemmed from a personal experience of this Irish insensitivity to animals when she first came to live in Dublin. From the window of her home, Patricia observed a man driving a donkey and cart down the street. The donkey was small and bony, his head drooping miserably, and the man was flaking him across the back with a thick stick, urging him to walk faster. Patricia was almost moved to tears at this sight and decided straightaway to write a story which would show that donkeys feel pain and experience exhaustion.

In *The Turf-Cutter's Donkey,* the two children, Seamus and

Eileen, come across a tinkers' encampment. They hide behind the bushes and watch, hoping they won't be spotted:

> A tall, ragged man with a bushy black beard and a bright yellow handkerchief twisted about his head was making a speech. At the end of every sentence he brought down a big stick on the back and sides of a donkey which was fastened to a tree. The children had never seen such a thin, miserable donkey before. It did not move even when it felt the stick, but stood still, its head hanging down, its long ears folded over each other. Its tail was like a bit of cord and its mane was all worn away.[9]

This pathetic sight horrifies the children, who determine to rescue the donkey from this cruelty. When they are discovered by the tinker chief, they throw him a silver teapot which they had found, the donkey makes a dash for freedom, Seamus and Eileen jump on his back, and they all escape together. From this beginning came three 'Turf-Cutter' books and the later book *Long Ears: The Story of a Little Grey Donkey*, all of which gave the donkey a vivid and loveable personality, heightened the public's awareness of the needs of animals, and made a strong case for the kinder treatment of donkeys, and of animals in general.

Patricia Lynch made no secret of her admiration for the nomadic lifestyle of the travelling people, but she took issue with their attitude to their animals. In an interview published in the magazine *The Cross*, she asserted that 'Tinkers have yet to learn that a kindly treated donkey is a good donkey.'[10] The donkey Long Ears bears out the truth of this statement. He is not the sentimental, idealised animal of some fiction, but a spirited, contrary beast who knows his own mind and gives love and loyalty to those who treat him kindly.

Writing about animals in a way that almost humanised them has long been popular in literature for children. Beatrix Potter gave her animals human features, dressing them up in various regalia and projecting human personalities on to them. Kenneth Grahame also created his own animal kingdom in *The Wind in the*

Willows, where the various animals vied for power and where their society was separate from, yet on a par with, human society, exhibiting all the same good and bad features. And of course Anna Sewell, who wrote *Black Beauty,* spent her life remonstrating against the thoughtless cruelty extended to ponies and horses in the newly industrialised Britain. In *Black Beauty,* the story is told from the horse's viewpoint and relates the different events and trials which made up Black Beauty's life.

In Patricia Lynch's case, the narrative voice is not that of the animal in question, but of its human companion. In *The Grey Goose of Kilnevin,* for instance, the little servant girl, Sheila, is the protagonist and Betsy the goose is her companion. Betsy does not take on a human form or speak with a human voice, but the two nevertheless have no difficulty in understanding one another's language. Where other people hear just a hiss and a gabble, Sheila hears a friend who can communicate with her – as we learn from the following passage. Betsy and Sheila have met up with the ballad singer and the boy, Fergus, who is carving the shape of a goose from a large potato:

> 'That's a quare goose!' says Betsy.
>
> Sheila clapped her hands in delight. 'Betsy can talk,' she cried.
>
> 'I've been talking all the time,' agreed the grey goose. 'Only ye had to taste the golden water before ye could understand me.'
>
> The Ballad Singer looked at Sheila in amazement.
>
> 'The crathure seems to know what ye're saying, girleen!' he exclaimed. 'But don't tell me you make sense of her hissing!'[11]

This world of extraordinary events and magical occurrences, interwoven with the harsh reality of the world of servant girls and homeless men, and children left to fend for themselves, is the unique creation of Patricia Lynch. There seems to be a common thread running through the backgrounds of many of the children's writers who produced 'animal' stories, however. A lonely or isolated childhood would appear to be the stimulus for producing narratives which show great sympathy with the animal world. Beatrix Potter, for instance, who created such believable characters in Flopsy, Mopsy, Cottontail and Peter, was brought up by parents who discouraged outside companionship. This threw her very much on to her own resources and helped develop her vivid imagination. For friendship, she had her pet menagerie – a rabbit, a hedgehog and a mouse – and these were later woven into her fiction. Enid Blyton – the most successful children's writer of the twentieth century (in her prime in the 1930s and 1940s, she produced up to fifty books a year, many of them 'animal' stories) – also had quite a lonely childhood. Her father abandoned the family when she was a young girl, and she had a difficult relationship with her mother. As a result, she was forced to live very much in her imagination and in the imaginative worlds she created.[12]

Patricia Lynch's stories undoubtedly alerted children of the 1940s and the 1950s – an era in Ireland when donkeys were beaten and frequently left unshod, where litters of pups and kittens were drowned without much thought, and where many children saw nothing wrong with raiding birds' nests and taking the eggs – to the fact that animals had feelings and that treating them with kindness and respect was no more than they deserved. She understood that, to quote the Dalai Lama: 'Life is as dear to a mute creature as it is to a man. Just as one wants happiness and fears pain, just as one wants to live and not die, so do other creatures.'[13] If Lynch had been around today, she may well have been involved in animal protection; certainly her stories have a concern with the environment that has only come to the fore in children's literature in very recent years.

13

THE WAR YEARS

There were shortages of many important commodities, including paper, across Europe in the wake of World War II. Publishers became more and more selective about what books they should take on, and how many copies of each they should print. Dent and Sons began to limit the publication and reprinting of certain books. Ireland's neutrality throughout the war had placed the country itself in a rather inward-looking situation. Ireland's most serious engagement with enemy planes was when, as a result of jammed radio signals, German warplanes went off course and bombed the North Strand area of Dublin on 30 May 1941, killing thirty-four people. Apart from this tragedy, Ireland's war suffering was on a more mundane scale than that of many other European nations, with internal transport disruption, fuel shortages, and food and energy rationing.

Eamon de Valera's Ireland, though materially constrained, was nonetheless rich culturally and spiritually, and the general atmosphere in the country seemed to lend itself naturally to an interest in tales and fables of Ireland's heroic past. Patricia Lynch, tuning in to this need, began to diversify her creative output. In 1943, the Irish religious publishers Burns and Oates approached her with a proposal to write a book about Irish saints. This would be Lynch's first book for adults. The idea appealed to her, but she first had to clear it with Dent, as her contract stated that she was not to produce competing work for another publisher. She wrote to Dent on 22 February 1943 asking for their approval and assuring them that the project would not compete with her main work for Dent – that it would indeed introduce her work to a new circle of readers. She went on to say that 'Just now when, owing to war conditions, you cannot bring out my books so frequently, this suggestion seems opportune.'[1] Dent replied that, since the proposed book was on such a specialised subject, and because Burns and Oates was a religious firm, there should be no conflict of interest. She duly received a contract from Burns and Oates dated 26 March 1943.

A substantial amount of time and research went into the preparation of this book, and Lynch in her bibliography cites such authors as Oliver St John Gogarty, Lady Gregory and Douglas Hyde. *Knights of God: Stories of the Irish Saints* was finally completed to her satisfaction and published in 1945. *Knights of God* was illustrated with wonderful, meticulously detailed drawings by the artist Alfred E. Kerr, who was later to illustrate two more of Patricia Lynch's books: *The Cobbler's Apprentice* and *Brogeen of the Stepping Stones,* both published in 1947. Kerr was an English-born artist who came to Belfast as a child. As a young man he became a member of Belfast Art Society, and took a keen interest in researching Celtic mythology and Gaelic culture. He wrote and illustrated many children's stories under the name of Patrick Sinclair and in 1936 and 1937 was chosen to design posters advertising tours of Northern Ireland by train and motor coach. The delicacy and beauty of his drawings earned him the title of 'The Ulster Beardsley' (a reference to the English artist Aubrey Beardsley, famous for his illustrations for an edition of Sir Thomas Malory's *Le Morte d'Arthur*). He very effectively captured the spirit of Lynch's work in *Knights of God,* where his illustrations possess a precision and delicacy reminiscent of the Book of Kells.

In *Knights of God,* which spans the era from the Romans up to the twelfth century, Lynch sets each saint against his or her relevant historical background through a narrative that is a mixture of history and legend. She portrays the saints as brave, adventurous men and women, full of kindness, humour and common sense, who spent their lives searching for spiritual truth. She begins her narrative with the strange tale of Saint Ciaran, a predecessor of Saint Patrick. Ciaran was reportedly born in 385; he sailed to Rome to join the early Christian church and eventually returned to Ireland to help Saint Patrick bring Christianity to the pagan Irish. The book goes on to explore the lives of Patrick, Enda, Brigid, Brendan, Columcille, Kevin, Laurence O'Toole, and finally Ethne. The book has been reprinted many times and is widely regarded as a classic of its kind. In 1955, the American publisher Regnery of Chicago brought it out; it was published in 1967 by the Bodley Head Press, London, and in 1971 appeared as a Puffin paperback. It was also the book choice of the Catholic Children's Book Club in New York.

The success of this book encouraged Patricia to start work on a collection of classical Irish folk tales. This collection was published by Clonmore & Reynolds in 1952 under the title *Tales of Irish Enchantment.* It was dedicated to Maud Gonne MacBride, and the illustrations were by Fergus O'Ryan. These folk tales had enriched Patricia's own childhood; by gathering them together in book form, she hoped that would be a source of inspiration for a whole new generation. Lynch never believed in being didactic in her writing. Indeed, she wrote in a magazine article: 'I do not want to preach. I want the story to tell its own lessons, just as the lives of the saints do.' In the same article, referring to *Tales of Irish Enchantment,* she said: 'I believe that these legends enshrine what is worth preserving in the early history and memory of the race.'[2] Patricia was always conscious of her responsibility towards her young readers and of the importance of passing on to them a rich inheritance of saga and folk history.

Two more collections of Lynch's short stories appeared in the 1940s. *Strangers at the Fair and Other Stories* was published by Browne and Nolan Ltd under their imprint the Richview Press in 1945. These charming, whimsical tales were illustrated by Westmeath artist Eileen Coghlan, who had attended the Metropolitan School of Art in Dublin and was also the illustrator of John D. Sheridan's *Paradise Alley,* Maura Laverty's *The*

Cottage on the Bog and Sinead de Valera's *Fairy Tales.* The same year, Gayfield Press of Dublin brought out a collection called *Lisheen at the Valley Farm and Other Stories,* which included work by the children's writer Helen Staunton and the Waterford playwright Teresa Deevy, as well as by Patricia Lynch.

Lynch's decision to move to publishers other than Dent was a practical one. At this stage, the royalties from her previous books were not huge, and although R.M.'s literary output was impressive, he was not making a great deal of money from journalism. Since Dent were cutting back their list because of paper shortages, and she needed to get her work published in order to make some money, she looked to other publishers. This is evident from the correspondence between Lynch and a Miss Eleanor Graham, an editor with Puffin Books. The two women had struck up a literary friendship, and on 31 December 1946 Miss Graham wrote to Patricia asking her about her situation with Dent:

> I know that keeping their Everyman Library going takes a great deal of their paper quota, but surely they manage to reprint some of your back work, don't they? And what about new books? I thought at first perhaps you were publishing with Nolan and Browne out of national loyalty – but is that all?

Patricia swiftly confirmed that 'It is not patriotism which made me go to Browne and Nolan but the desire to be published.'[3]

As well as contacting Irish publishers, Lynch approached the London publishers Hollis and Carter to reissue *The Cobbler's Apprentice* in 1947 (it had first been published in 1931 by The Talbot Press of Dublin) and Ker-Cross Publishing Co. of London to bring out *Brogeen of the Stepping Stones,* also in 1947. Both these books were beautifully illustrated with black-and-white drawings by Alfred Kerr. The latter book introduced the character of Brogeen, the mischievous, sometimes cantankerous

111

leprechaun who was to become the hero of at least twelve full-length books by Patricia. Here, as the narrative begins, we are introduced to Brogeen in this dramatic fashion:

> Not far from the bridge with seven arches which crosses the river below Flat-Top Mountain, lived a shoemaker and his name was Brogeen.
> He made shoes so small your thumb would fill one. He had a hammer with a golden head and he wore a leather apron fastened by a golden buckle, for Brogeen was a leprechaun.[4]

In fact, Brogeen (from the Irish for 'little shoe') was a leprechaun who was to become world-famous. His later escapades were to be dramatised by the BBC, serialised by RTÉ and translated into many languages. He was particularly popular with the French, who called him 'Korik', the Breton word for a small gnomish creature. In relation to this book, Lynch defended herself against charges of relying overmuch on fantasy for her subject matter by observing that 'there can be nothing more fantastic than Ireland's world of sea and sky, of red sunsets and golden moons. Yet if among the waving white bog cotton, *canavaun*, I spy just one little leprechaun, people who accepted all the other wonders as "ordinary" think that this is most fantastic. It is time we saw life as a whole and realized its magic.'[5] Patricia herself had a wonderful capacity for seeing and appreciating the magic of nature and of life in general. Her own sense of adventure meant that for her, each new day was a doorway to a new world. She loved to travel, she loved her home, she loved food, she loved her garden. She was never bored, and therefore was never boring.

By far the most important book that Patricia Lynch wrote in the 1940s was the autobiographical *A Storyteller's Childhood*, published by Dent and Sons in 1947. In this book, dedicated 'To the Good

Days', she gave a dramatic account of her childhood. In keeping with the tone of so many of her fictional narratives, this childhood was one of magic, adventure and joy, and perhaps even fantasy. There is no sentimentality or self-pity in her account, but instead a strange detachment when recounting the feelings of the little girl who was forced to leave her home in Cork so early in her life, and then taken here, there and everywhere as necessity demanded. *A Storyteller's Childhood* is the story of a loving and very adaptable child who accepted her lot and never questioned the fact that she was abandoned to friends, relations and boarding schools while her mother and brother pursued their quest for their inheritance. There is never a hint of blame in this account, and no dimming of the love that she felt for her widowed mother. In Patricia's view, Nora had done what she felt she had to do, and if this meant a less-than-ideal childhood for her daughter, it was the price that had to be paid, and was nobody's fault.

When *A Storyteller's Childhood* first appeared, some of the reviews were less than flattering. The *Times Literary Supplement* of 27 December 1947 gave the following account:

It is true that the Irishry is rather too strong in the earlier chapters, which are full of peat sellers and wishing wells and delightful old women too good to be true: perhaps this is because a great deal of it can scarcely be genuine recollection but must be largely built up of single remembered pictures strung together by imagination and by information acquired later in life. The author had the sort of childhood which all the books on child psychology say is the worst possible – no sense of security, no fixed home background, no steady education and constant separation from the mother and brother who made up the only element of continuity and of home in her life. Such an upbringing may well be disastrous for certain types of character; yet for a child with well-defined creative gifts it provides food for the imagination and emotional tension which brings it into flower. . . . Yet out of this she has constructed a tale which is as happy and pleasing as her own children's stories.

Though ever so slightly patronising, this is a remarkably shrewd insight into how Patricia Lynch turned her upbringing to advantage, both as a person and as a creative writer. She had mastered the ability to stand outside her own life and observe it, and later to re-create these observations in her narrative.

Other reviews were more enthusiastic. *Irish Writing,* in its issue of April 1948, states:

> Her story reads like a fairy tale . . . an unlocking of a treasury of sights, sounds, incidents and characters . . . She leans over the wall of years that separates her from her childhood and sees Tricia as a person distinct in time and surroundings, and Tricia is a remarkable person.

The book was very popular. Eric Forbes-Boyd, writing in the *Sunday Times* of 28 December 1947, compared the story to accounts of the wanderings of Oisín or Homer's *Odyssey,* and said it was in the tradition of the 'best celtic [*sic*] magic'. It struck a chord with rural and city readers alike and was a big hit with the Irish-immigrant population in America and Britain, where it attained a cult-like following.

Distribution in Northern Ireland was more problematic. To send books from the south to the north required an import licence from the British Board of Trade. In December 1947, the representative of the distributors in Ireland, Browne and Nolan, wrote to Dent and Sons that *A Storyteller's Childhood* was selling well in the Republic but that the position with regard to Northern Ireland was very different, mainly because of difficulties with distributors. The publisher had lobbied the UK Board of Trade, which had contacted the British customs authorities, who had then been in touch with the relevant Departments of State in Ireland, but all to no avail. This situation was made even more ludicrous by the anomalies in the system. Books sent north of the border by parcel post were being let through, but bulk importation was being held up; as a result, Browne and Nolan were sending supplies by post to each individual bookseller in Northern Ireland. The letter ends on a rather apologetic note, assuring Dent and Sons that 'We shall do everything possible to ensure that the book is on sale in Northern Ireland at the earliest moment.'[6]

Dent and Sons were fortunate to acquire the services of the artist Harry Kernoff to illustrate *A Storyteller's Childhood;* his striking black-and-white drawings captured the heart and soul of the narrative. Kernoff was born in London of Jewish parents but moved to Dublin with his family when he was fourteen. He attended night classes at the Dublin Metropolitan School of Art, where he became the first student to win the Taylor Scholarship – the person deciding who would win the scholarship being Jack B. Yeats. After a spell in Paris, Kernoff threw himself into his work as an artist, producing genre paintings, landscapes, portraits, woodcuts, abstract paintings, illustrations for numerous publications, and stage sets for various theatrical productions. Kernoff was greatly influenced by the Russian Futurists: he visited the Soviet Union in 1930 – R. M. Fox had done the same in 1921 – as part of an Irish delegation led by Hannah Sheehy-Skeffington. He spent six weeks there, and in Moscow he had meetings with members of the Association of Revolutionary Artists, who saw artists as the 'spokesmen of the people's spiritual life'. All these remarkable influences show through in the sombre, character-driven illustrations for *A Storyteller's Childhood,* and add great weight to the narrative. The fact that she secured the services of such an important artist is a telling indication of the esteem in which Lynch's work was held in the late 1940s.

Maurice MacGonigal, the landscape artist who was professor of painting at the Royal Hibernian Academy of Arts from 1947 to 1978, was to describe Kernoff as 'a little genius'; his genius is evident in these illustrations, which reflect so vividly the tone of the narrative. Kernoff received the sum of £65 for his illustrations for the book.

One other book of Patricia Lynch's which was published in the 1940s was *The Mad O'Haras,* which Dent and Sons brought out in 1948. Dent had on one occasion suggested to the author that, in her books, she should 'have more realism and less fantasy, so as to appeal to English children';[7] with *The Mad O'Haras,* Patricia certainly complied with this request. It is a children's novel devoid of even a hint of fantasy – a powerful story firmly grounded in reality, and demonstrating the skill of the author in its fast-moving narrative and well-defined characters. Grania O'Hara, a budding teenage artist, leaves her home in the village of Dromard, where she lives with an aunt and an uncle, to find her mother in Castle O'Hara, a crumbling, Gothic-style castle inhabited by some very eccentric characters.

The plot would be controversial by today's terms, dealing as it does with the feuds between the settled community and travellers, but once again the search for home, family and identity is central. The O'Haras are shunned by the locals because Grania's grandmother had 'run away from a decent farm to take up with a rovin' tinker'.[8] As a result, it was felt in the small, insular community that, even at two generations removed, 'bad blood' ran in the veins of all the O'Haras. The story is rumbustious and lively, with strong characterisation and vivid dialogue, and is aimed at a slightly older child than many of Patricia's stories. A French reviewer praised it, saying that 'The Irish character, which mingles dreams, poetry and great good sense, lives in these people so well described by a romantic who understands her art so well.'[9]

The Mad O'Haras was one of the author's favourite books, and was well received abroad as well as in Ireland. Page of Boston published it under the title *Grania of Castle O'Hara* in 1952, and more recently Poolbeg Press brought it out in 1997 as part of their Children's Classics series: evidence of its continuing popularity with today's children. In October 1958, *The Mad O'Haras* was made into a six-part television series, starring Jacqueline Ryan, by the BBC.

The English artist Elizabeth Rivers was commissioned to illustrate *The Mad O'Haras*. Rivers was a daring choice to illustrate this book; her strong, earthy drawings are particularly effective. Rivers, who was born in Hertfordshire in England, spent much of her life in Ireland, on Inis Mór in the Aran Islands and later in Dalkey, County Dublin. She had studied in London in the Royal Academy School and was greatly influenced by her tutor, the renowned artist Walter Sickert, who was himself a pupil of Whistler. She later studied in Paris, and on her return to England became a member of an avant-garde group of artists called 'The Twenties Group'. Other artists in this group were Norah McGuinness and Barbara Hepworth. She moved to Inis Mor in 1935, and became very interested in the landscape and life of the people there. While there, she wrote a book called *Stranger in Aran,* adorning it with her own drawings, and this was published by the Cuala Press – which was owned by the Yeats sisters, Lily and Lollie. Dent, and Patricia Lynch herself, were very honoured to have an artist of the calibre of Elizabeth Rivers to take on the commission to illustrate *The Mad O'Haras,* but considering the litany of wonderful artists who had gone before her in contributing to Patricia Lynch's fame, she was in good company.

By the close of the 1940s, Lynch was acclaimed for the quality of her work, and her books were widely read. The Library Association suggested that she be awarded the Carnegie Medal for her services to literature, but because she was not a British citizen she was not deemed eligible. In 1949, however, the *Junior Bookshelf,* an English journal catering for children's librarians, brought out a special Patricia Lynch issue. This was devoted entirely to the Irish writer and included pictures from all her books, as well as excerpts and articles. The playwright Teresa Deevy, author of *The King of Spain's Daughter,* was a prominent contributor to this issue. Many years later, for Christmas 1955, Deevy sent a signed copy of *The King of Spain's Daughter* to Patricia and R.M., with the inscription 'This little booklet is for two very good friends whose interest in my work is a joy to me. With best wishes and my love.'[10] Patricia saw this special issue of *Junior Bookshelf* as a sort of consolation prize for not being able to accept the Carnegie Medal.

14

Two Books a Year

Now in her fifties, Patricia Lynch had reached the pinnacle of her success as a writer. She and R.M. had developed a wonderfully supportive partnership of encouragement and mental stimulation. Their marriage had produced no children, but their pleasure in one another's company and their self-sufficiency and creativity almost certainly compensated for this. Patricia loved children, but she never, publicly at any rate, expressed any deep longings to have a child herself. All her creative energies were poured into her books, and each child character she created became real and precious to her. Her own needs and desires were simple, and R.M., who loved her deeply, saw to it that nothing got in the way of the continuous flow of her creativity.

Lynch was now completing books at the rate of two a year, as well as contributing to numerous magazines, newspapers, and radio programmes. The couple also had their Wednesday 'At Home' days, when they held open house for other writers, poets and theatre personalities. Most of the people who came on these days were acquaintances of R.M.'s, but his friends were her friends, and after they had met Patricia, people were immediately captivated by her. She had a mischievous sense of humour, and an impish and rather naive attitude to life, but underneath all this she held strong convictions and kept herself well informed of the events of the time. She was also very socially conscious, and as she matured as a writer, this came through in her stories. The problems associated with emigration, the treatment of itinerants, the population move from rural to urban areas, the need for better educational facilities, the plight of children who were isolated from the mainstream because of some physical handicap – all these were woven into the fabric of her stories in a non-didactic way.

Dent was still her main publisher, but in February 1950 the company declined to accept more than one book a year from her. Dent also began to chip away at the sums which she could expect to get in royalties. On 5 June 1950, Dent wrote to Patricia informing her that:

> We have under consideration the question of a reprint of *Fiddler's Quest*. Unfortunately sales of this title are not as good as some of your other books. At the current price of eight shillings and sixpence this shows no profit margins at all. . . . Would you accept a reduction in the royalty to ten percent of the published price?

Patricia replied that this was altogether too drastic. 'I have climbed slowly from a starting royalty of five percent, and during the war period my returns were very low,' she wrote on 10 June 1950. She goes on to emphasise that 'I do feel that to forego royalties, which are the legitimate reward of such success as my books have attained, is a serious matter, not only financially but also affecting my status as a writer.[1] Lynch's confidence in her own work was now such that she could afford to question the decisions of her publishers. She had compromised more than once during the difficult war-time years, when she was well aware of the problems being experienced by the publishing industry. She now felt, however, that it was time to move on: she began to look around for another publisher.

In 1951, Dent brought out *The Dark Sailor of Youghal*, illustrated by Jerome Sullivan. This is an eerie tale of a ghostly silver ship, the *Santa Maria*, which lured sailors to their death. It had historical connections, based as it was on a legendary tale of Philip of Youghal, who had gone to sea with Christopher Columbus and was doomed to sail the seven seas for eternity.

This book is also, in a sense, a reworking of the legend of Tír na nÓg. *The Dark Sailor of Youghal* tells the story of Nial Burke, a motherless boy who sets off to search for his father, Brendan; his father has been lured away by the strange Dark Sailor. As in so many of Lynch's stories, the hunger for foreign places is interwoven with the quest and the search for home, family and security. The story ends on a moral note, with the spell being broken when Nial and his companions use their free will to rescue the inhabitants of the ghost ship, thereby releasing Brendan Burke.

Jerome Sullivan's sombre drawings add to the other-worldly quality of this narrative. Sullivan had also illustrated *The Seventh Pig,* a collection of short stories by Lynch which was originally published by Dent in 1950 and was re-issued, with the addition of one extra story, 'The Fourth Man', under the title *The Black Goat of Slievemore and Other Irish Fairy Tales* in 1959. This book was dedicated 'To Mrs Hennessy'. The additional story had been chosen by David Marcus, the near-legendary discoverer of talented Irish short-story writers, for publication on 11 January 1954 in issue No. 25 of the magazine *Irish Writing,* of which he was editor. He paid Patricia four guineas – a substantial sum of money at that time – for the story.

In 1952, Dent published Lynch's *The Boy at the Swinging Lantern,* which tells the tale of the displaced Rory, who searches for his roots and finds that his background is not what he had expected. This adventure story, which contains plenty of twists and turns, appealed to a more discriminating audience. There were shades of Patricia's own youth in this narrative, with the ongoing search for the mysterious Mr Blanchard and the legacy of Timothy Patrick Lynch's business interests in Egypt being echoed in Rory's search for his real ancestry and his ultimate discovery of the unexpected.

Joan Kiddell-Monroe captured the spirit of *The Boy at the Swinging Lantern* in her shadowy black-and-white drawings and her mysterious-looking figures. Kiddell-Monroe, who was used extensively by British publishers of children's books, excelled in illustrations for books of fairy stories and legends. Over the years, she illustrated volumes of Scottish, French, German, African, Indian, Chinese, Russian and Scandinavian folk tales and legends collected by various writers. She had illustrated Lynch's book *Long Ears* in 1943, and would go on to illustrate three more of Patricia's books.

In 1952, Patricia's second publisher, Burke and Co. of London, brought out their first book in the 'Brogeen' series, *Brogeen Follows the Magic Tune.* This was to prove the beginning of a very fruitful relationship between Lynch and this publisher: in all, Burke brought out twelve novels featuring Brogeen, the querulous yet lovable leprechaun. The Brogeen series related the adventures of the fairy folk who lived in the Fort of Sheen. These were a mixture of 'little people', comprising leprechauns, phoukas, banshees and the like; Brogeen, being the shoemaker for the whole fairy community, is kept busy. The Fort of Sheen straddled two worlds – the land of youth, or Tír na nÓg, and the world of human folk. Lynch portrays the tension and even enmity that she saw as existing between the two worlds.

Although Brogeen has everything he could want in the land of the 'Good People', he is constantly yearning for new experiences and is forever venturing out into the human world. On one such trip, Brogeen meets up with the fiddler Batt Kelly, and they strike up a strange friendship. Brogeen is too soft-hearted for his own good: he allows Batt to follow him into the fort one stormy night – something no human has ever been allowed to do – and gives him access to the magic tune. Because of this, Brogeen is banished from the fort and sent out into the human world to retrieve the magic tune.

The leprechaun takes on all sorts of challenges in this fast-moving, richly imaginative story, which taps into folklore and legend, as well as presenting the reader with an assortment of charming and believable characters. The British artist Peggy Fortnum captures the frenetic activity of the plot and the whimsical nature of the protagonist in her fluid drawings. Fortnum was one of the leading illustrators of children's books in her day and also, like Lynch, a richly imaginative writer. Indeed, her own childhood, narrated in a memoir called *Running Wild*,[2] was as fractured and unsettled as Patricia's. Fortnum was to become famous as the illustrator of the 'Paddington Bear' series, as well as of Kenneth Grahame's *The Reluctant Dragon*.

In 1966, a Brogeen book in German translation was broadcast on Swiss radio, and excerpts from the book were broadcast on Berlin radio, confirming the international popularity of this appealing character. In 1969, RTÉ was to produce a puppet-based television serial based on the book, with the same title: *Brogeen Follows the Magic Tune*. This series was very popular and sparked a renewed interest in all the Brogeen novels.

Patricia Lynch now had two publishers, Dent and Burke. Incredible as it may seem, she produced a book a year for each of them up to the mid 1960s. In 1953, she published *Brogeen and the Green Shoes* with Burke, again illustrated by Peggy Fortnum. This book once more relates the adventures of the fairy shoemaker. There is a wonderful normality about the fantasy in this story: the green shoes take off on their own, followed by the wayward Brogeen, whose curiosity about the world is stronger than the ties which bind him to the fairy fort. Brogeen's kindness to all those he meets is rewarded a hundredfold, and the story has a happy ending when he returns safely to his own little home:

> He stepped inside and closed the door. His little brown teapot was hot. His blue cup and saucer were ready on the table. The kettle began to sing.[3]

What more could any leprechaun want? This tale was a huge favourite with younger children, who could readily identify with Brogeen's trials in the world of 'big' people.

Lynch's book for Dent in 1953 went under the wonderful title of *Delia Daly of Galloping Green*. The book was illustrated once again by Joan Kiddell-Monroe and was dedicated 'To the Other Delia'. *Delia Daly of Galloping Green* avoided any hint of fantasy or myth and instead addressed some serious issues of the time. It is set in the village of Dunooka in County Cork, a village similar to those with which Patricia would have been familiar from her childhood. In such villages, very little happened to alleviate the day-to-day monotony, but families and communities were closely involved with each other.

The tale deals with the Daly family, who own a small shop in the village. There are four children, who are happy and carefree, and satisfied with their lot – meagre though it may seem by today's standards. Then along comes wealthy cousin Kate, who offers to send one of the girls to boarding school. Naturally, this results in jealousy among the siblings. Delia, the youngest girl, thinks she should be the one chosen because she is the most intelligent. But cousin Kate opts for Nuala, who then goes off to become a boarder in the school in Dublin, far away from the little village of Dunooka.

In this poignant tale of poor Nuala, who is utterly miserable in her new surroundings, Lynch draws on her own memories of being uprooted from the security of home and family, of the loneliness of being away from home, and of the rivalry and bitchiness which can exist in an all-girls boarding school. The story also deals with favouritism within families, as Delia tries in vain to fill the gap left in her parents' lives by Nuala's departure.

It is a story full of twists and surprises, and with characters with which the reader can empathise easily. Although the setting is now somewhat dated, the story is universal and timeless, and presented with a freshness which makes it relevant to any age. Lynch's plots can sometimes seem deceptively simple, but underneath is a deep awareness of the vagaries of human nature and a strong tolerance for, and understanding of, the pettiness of which we are all capable. Moreover, the moral message that is contained in many of her stories is never conveyed in a preachy manner. Overall, *Delia Daly of Galloping Green* has stood the test of time very well: it can hold its own with many children's classics, past or present.

On 11 November 1953, Dent's American agent, one Marion

Saunders of 104 East Fortieth Street, wrote to E. F. Bozman of Dent regarding *Delia Daly of Galloping Green,* saying that she had now read the book and regarded it as 'very Irish'. She wanted to take it on, however, and would 'like to have copies of any good British reviews, outstanding sales figures, or anything else which might help us in our "sales talk".'[4] In fact, *Delia Daly* proved to be a good, steady seller, so Ms Saunders' interest was more than justified.

In 1954, Patricia Lynch produced *Brogeen and the Bronze Lizard* for Burke Publishing. The book was illustrated by Grace Golden – this being the only occasion on which this particular illustrator was used. Golden was born in 1904 and studied at the Chelsea School of Art and the Royal College of Art; she was a well-known painter, illustrator and poster designer. For Dent, Patricia wrote *Orla of Burren;* Joan Kiddell-Monroe was once again chosen to illustrate it. This tale of fantasy and adventure draws heavily on Lynch's own knowledge and love of Irish history and folklore, and was a particular favourite of hers. The protagonists, Orla, Standish and Miles, holidaying at a farmhouse close to an enchanted mountain, find a magic stone which transports them back in time to the sixteenth century.

Although this device has been used in many children's stories, in this case there is a particularly Irish slant to the narrative. The landscape in which the children find themselves is that of the west of Ireland at the time of the famous female pirate Granuaile. Grace or Grania O'Malley was the daughter of the sea captain and pirate Owen O'Malley, who sailed the high seas around Ireland and Scotland, and south to the English Channel. His beautiful daughter Grania travelled with him and learned from him to be brave and fearless, to handle a sword with the best of them, and to command a ship and its crew. When he died, she became chief of the O'Malley clan. She built towers all along the western seaboard to protect her people from invasion.

In Lynch's story, the children become completely caught up in this sixteenth-century world, with its dramas of battles and chieftains and dark deeds at sea, of looting, pillage and destruction. The book is a historical drama but is most of all a story of brave little Orla, who, like her creator, craves both adventure and stability, and for whom the homecoming is always the ultimate goal. In *Orla of Burren,* Lynch draws not only on the Irish historical past but also on the stories she had been told about members of her own family: her Uncle Henry, who had been lost at sea, and her father, who had taken off across the world and never returned.

The following year, 1955, Lynch produced two very significant books: for Burke, *Brogeen and the Princess of Sheen,* which was illustrated by Christopher Brooker, and for Dent, *Tinker Boy,* illustrated by Harry Kernoff. *Brogeen and the Princess of Sheen* tells the story of the fairy princess who wishes she could be human, and whose wish comes true. Brogeen is sent to rescue her from her fate – a task which he resents, but which produces some hilarious and touching results. This is a story much loved by both young children, who easily relate to the naughty princess, and by adults, who find the language musical and flowing, and ideal for reading aloud.

The second book, *Tinker Boy,* touches on several very important issues of the time. In the Ireland of the 1950s one particular form of racism was undeniably present – against members of the travelling community. By this time, tinsmiths were a thing of the past in Irish society, and the arrival of members of the travelling community into towns and villages was greeted with resentment and fear. The travellers were regarded by many as noisy, feckless idlers, and very little attempt was made by settled communities to understand their ways or their culture.

Sometimes, groups of travelling families would settle for the winter months in lay-bys outside towns, and then their children might be sent to the local school. Naturally, these children were at a distinct disadvantage, having had only the most sporadic educational opportunities. Although the national schools could not refuse to take them – under the Irish Constitution, then as now, all children are entitled to an education – there was a great reluctance to accept them, and their presence created tensions in the schools in question. In *Tinker Boy,* Lynch challenges these preconceptions and undermines the assumption that there could be no integration between the two cultures.

Tessa Nolan, living with her parents and brothers in the fictional village of Danesford, is a kind and soft-hearted girl. One morning, she wakes up to the sound of clattering hooves, as a band of tinkers arrives to camp on Black Boar Common. On her way to school, Tessa takes a short cut through the common; the sight which meets her is one which was common enough around villages in Ireland of the 1950s:

> Bony horses grazed and furtive-looking dogs slunk restlessly. . . . Fires in buckets flared and smoked. Untidy women were sitting on boxes drinking tea, men lounged against carts smoking, boys and girls sat on the ground biting hungrily at thick hunks of bread. The crying of babies rose and mingled with the chattering of the starlings.[5]

When one of the tinker women addresses Tessa, she immediately feels afraid – which, after all, is the emotion that people are expected to feel in the presence of tinkers. But because Tessa has been well brought up, she replies to the tinker woman, telling her her name and where her school is. The woman's son, Dara MacDara, is the same age as Tessa, so Tessa is asked if she will bring him along with her to the school. The boy's clothes are tattered and his feet are bare, but Tessa thinks that he is the most dignified boy she has ever met.

She takes him with her to school – where the reaction to him is as Tessa would have expected it to be: the teacher looks scornful and the other pupils giggle and stare. When Dara is given a desk beside Tessa's brother, Michael Joe, the boy declares that he is not going to have a tinker sitting beside him. All the other children follow his example, and spread out so that there is nowhere for Dara to sit.

Tessa, ashamed of the rudeness of her brother and her classmates, makes room for Dara at her desk. She shares her copy-book, her pencils and her books with him and helps him to find his way around the lessons. In a very short time, both the children and their teacher discover that Dara is no demon but just another little boy, no better or no worse than the rest of them – in fact, probably amongst the brightest in the class. A simple gesture of friendship has helped break down the prejudice of a whole village. Soon the tinker families are accepted as a colourful part of the community, and for their season on Black Boar Common, mutual rights are respected. As Aunt Teresa declares at the end of the book: 'Tinkers and gardas, shopkeepers and schoolchildren, we're all the same.'[6] The narrative fairly gallops along, and Lynch's own secret admiration for the flamboyant, devil-may-care lifestyle of the Irish travellers of her childhood is never far from the surface. Of course, Harry Kernoff's striking coloured frontispiece and his strong black-and-white illustrations perfectly complement the text.

The Bookshop on the Quay, which Dent brought out in 1956, illustrated by Peggy Fortnum, again tackles some important social issues. According to Patricia, the story, which is set in Dublin, was inspired by the sight of a tiny, shabby-looking second-hand bookshop which she sometimes passed by on her way to and from the city. It started her wondering about the owner of such a premises, and how a living could be made from such a small stock. It also set her thinking of her own childhood, and of her grandfather's boast that he had never been known to pass by a bookshop without stopping, browsing and buying. Shane, the protagonist in this story, has much in common with Lynch herself. He is a runaway orphan on a quest to find his Uncle Tim, on whom he pins his hopes of a brighter future. The book is set in the Dublin of the 1950s: the city is depicted as being very close to its rural roots, and the smells and sounds, and values, of rural Ireland are woven into the text.

Shane comes from west Cork, and the elusive Uncle Tim is

a cattle drover who 'could do anything he wished with animals and was the best drover between Cork and Limerick.'[7] The setting for the story, though undeniably Dublin, could be any rural market town: much of the action takes place around Smithfield Market, where the farmers come to buy and sell their beasts.

Shane, wandering around the market area in his fruitless search for his uncle, eventually ends up gazing into the window of 'The Four Masters' Bookshop' on Ormond Quay. His hungry and bedraggled look attracts the attention of Eilís O'Clery, the bookseller's wife, herself a countrywoman. She invites Shane to join her family for supper, and he ends up moving in with the family, working in the bookshop and sharing a room with their son Patrick. Shane settles in very well in the little bookshop, but when he eventually finds his Uncle Tim and is offered the opportunity to return to his rural background, he is faced with a difficult choice. He has fallen in love with the city but also has a hankering to return to his roots in west Cork:

> Shane stood gazing at the lighted bridges and the high dark buildings beyond the river . . . to go back, to watch Maggie's eyes growing big with wonder, to have the boys think him a hero and a traveller, to hand round the presents he had bought.[8]

His dilemma is solved for him when Mr O'Clery suggests that he go home with Uncle Tim and stay there for a holiday, but then return to Dublin to his job in the bookshop and to his adoptive family.

'We will come back to Dublin, won't we, Uncle Tim?' asks Shane at the close of the narrative. 'We will, lad. We will. Doesn't the whole world come back to Dublin?' his uncle answers.[9]

Shane has succeeded in his search for a family and has satisfied his urge for travel and adventure. Lynch has once again drawn on her own life to produce a vivid, challenging story.

The review of *The Bookshop on the Quay* that appeared in the *Times Literary Supplement* of 23 November 1956 includes high praise for the illustrator, Peggy Fortnum. The reviewer writes:

> So many different artists have tried to catch the atmosphere of Miss Lynch's prose – only Peggy Fortnum has fully succeeded. Her sketches of children, haunched, springing, dishevelled, against half-seen surroundings, are exactly right.

In the same year, 1956, Patricia wrote *Brogeen and the Lost Castle,* which was published by Burke and which once again featured the adventures of the inimitable Brogeen and his own quest for adventure. This book was illustrated by Christopher Brooker, who illustrated many children's books for Burke. In October 1957, BBC's *Children's Hour* broadcast the story in six instalments – in an adaptation by Charles Witherspoon, who did much work for the BBC – thereby enabling an even wider audience to enjoy the adventures of the appealing leprechaun Brogeen.

15

Living and Writing

Patricia Lynch's enormous creative output was matched by that of her husband, R. M. Fox. In many respects, however, he put her talents before his own. For one thing, he typed all her manuscripts. She wrote her novels and short stories in longhand on the desk in the room which was assigned as her study, but truth to tell, she was not fussy where the writing took place. In an interview with journalist Christine Crowley, Patricia was asked what were the best conditions for a writer, and she answered that 'One must have time to write, lack of money may be a spur but too much anxiety is bad. The real writer will usually triumph over conditions. I must have quietness to write and I have tried to arrange my life so that telephone and visitors don't interrupt – a time for society and a time for solitude.' She went on to describe her writing methods:

> A book usually starts with characters and place. As it goes on, the plot evolves. Sometimes I think about people and sometimes I wonder about a place and read about its history, trying to soak up its atmosphere – this gives me a plan but not too rigid. I find my characters everywhere but chiefly among what might be called the 'ordinary people' who express their emotions, and not those drawing-room folk who, as Yeats once put it, say nothing but gaze into the fire.[1]

After she had shaped a story in a first draft, Patricia gave it to R.M. to read. She said that her husband was the first critic of all her work, and she trusted his judgement. R.M. would then correct her spellings – spelling was never her strong point – and afterwards he would take the manuscript and type it on his old-fashioned typewriter before sending it off to one of her publishers or to any of the various magazines to which Patricia was a regular contributor. R.M. also dealt with most of the business side of her writing, covering disputes with publishers over royalties, organising her tax affairs, dealing with translators and foreign rights to her work, arranging interviews, and replying to her business letters. In effect, he acted as a kind of agent for her, while still pursuing his own work.

As Lynch's profile as a children's author grew, she began to attract more and more publicity. In 1952, Katherine C. Lloyd, the illustrator for *King of the Tinkers,* was commissioned by Dent to do a pastel portrait of Patricia. This portrait was first shown at a party given by Dent in the author's honour in London in August 1952. R.M. and Patricia travelled to England for this party. Many distinguished writers and artists attended, and the occasion was profiled in *Social and Personal* magazine. Patricia, although she tended to be an unassuming character, relished such occasions and took a childlike delight in meeting other creative people. Such people responded warmly to her and often corresponded with her, even reporting to her on the progress of their own careers. In July 1955, for instance, one such friend, the artist Harry Kernoff, who had illustrated *A Storyteller's Childhood* and *Tinker Boy,* wrote to her and sent her a beautiful book entitled *Thirty-six Woodcuts by Harry Kernoff RHA,* with the inscription 'To Patricia Lynch and R. M. Fox'.

Patricia did not accept all the invitations she received, however. In 1954, she was asked to fly to New York for a book launch but turned down the invitation, explaining that 'I have too much gardening to do!'[2]

R.M. kept up a stream of correspondence of his own with people whom he met on his trips abroad and with the many editors, publishers and writers with whom he was in contact. The broad spectrum of both his and Patricia's contacts is illuminated by a letter, dated 6 June 1956, which he received from a Franz Fromme of Bremen, Germany, who wrote:

Since 1953 I have been receiving [the magazine] *Ireland of the Welcomes*. I was with you [Fox] in 1939 when I planned a German edition of your wife's *Fairy Tales*. But the Nazis – they instructed me that they wished to avoid the disgrace of England, and therefore books on Irish freedom would not be allowed in Hitler's Germany.[3]

Fromme seems to have enjoyed both R.M.'s socialist pamphlets and Patricia's tales of myth and legend. Perhaps he was planning a trip to Ireland to attend one of R.M. and Patricia's Wednesday afternoon parties, where a *cead míle fáilte* would await him.

During this period, R.M. and Patricia travelled whenever and wherever they could. R.M. wrote many travel articles for various magazines and journals, which necessitated trips around Ireland and abroad. Work assignments, book launches, publicity tours – every chance they got, they were off. Patricia loved the thrill of being on the move, and the sense of excitement she felt on arriving in a new place never left her. But it was, as she said, 'always wonderful to come back and feel that, if we don't stir a step outside the country, we are in one of the loveliest places in the world.'[4]

On several occasions, the couple went back to Cork – where Patricia tried, but failed, to find her old house in Sunday's Well. Patricia always described Cork as 'the dream city of her youth' and said that it was a city which had everything: 'quays, hilly streets, a glorious river leading one way to the mountains, the other to the ocean, the glamour of Blackrock Castle and the music of Shandon.'[5]

One of the biggest thrills of her life, according to Patricia, was when she discovered that her native city had honoured her by placing a picture of her, with some information about her background and work, in the 'hall of fame' in Fitzgerald's Park in Cork. In an unpublished article entitled 'Ireland of the Young', she said: 'I must confess to a twinge of pride when I saw the features of the girl from Fair Hill gazing at me from the wall.'[6]

In 1956, R.M. undertook an arduous journey which did not include Patricia. The Chinese Association for Cultural Relations invited a delegation of two women and six men from Ireland to visit the People's Republic of China, which at that time was rarely visited by Westerners. Fox was a member of the delegation, which included educationalists, sculptors and artists, as well as other writers. Their mission was to see and report their findings on schools, universities, arts, crafts and cultural life in the new People's Republic, which had been set up in 1949. The twenty-thousand-mile journey took three days and two nights from London, by boat, overland and rail. The two sculptors, John Bourke and Hilary Heron, were particularly interested in the structure of the Great Wall of China.

Patricia could not accompany her husband on this occasion, since spouses were not allowed to accompany the delegates. She missed him desperately, writing him many letters and counting the days until his return. In her letters, she kept him informed of all that was going on at home, of everyday events in Dublin, of the weather, and of any little ailments which she had. She also gave him stern advice as to what he was and what not to eat on this exotic tour. Patricia was always interested in food: her books are littered with descriptions of it, and all her protagonists find solace in sitting down to a good meal. A journalist, Jane Healy, had once remarked that Patricia Lynch, along with Maura Laverty, the author of various novels and cookery books. was one of the most food-obsessed writers in Irish literature![7] R.M. seems to have ignored her advice, however, since he describes in a letter to her eating everything he was offered while on the trip, without experiencing any ill-effects.

R.M., conscious of how lonely his wife would be without him, had arranged for Amy Holland, a close friend of his since his time in Ruskin College, to keep Patricia company in his absence. A letter from Amy to R.M. during this time is indicative of the love and affection which Patricia inspired in all who had any dealings with her. The letter, dated 20 September 1956, reads:

Dear Dick,

Patricia is a mixture of child, fairy and wise woman. She is a fascinating woman, and how you managed to capture her heart I don't know. It must have been fool's luck – you are a lucky fellow and that's the truth. If I get any complaints from Patricia I shall fly over and land you one. You have to walk slowly with her, and not rush her. . . . Surround her with your love.

Affectionately,
Amy.[8]

While in China, Fox and his party visited workshops making jade and ivory carvings, and a cotton factory in Peking (now Beijing). Through the group's interpreter, Fox discovered that Chinese trade-union officials at the cotton factory were very interested in his *History of the Irish Citizen Army* and in the part played by the Irish labour defence force during the great strike of 1913 and in the later struggle for national independence. Fox draws a comparison between the movement inspired by Larkin in Dublin in 1913 and the 1922 struggle of the Chinese peasants and railwaymen against the corrupt warlords. Another visit took the delegation to the slums of Shanghai, where they witnessed the appalling opium problem. They also visited the Peking Opera Theatre and saw a performance of Romeo and Juliet. The Shaw centenary had been celebrated there a few weeks before, with productions from Ibsen, Shaw and Oscar Wilde, as well as Shakespeare; the playwright Lennox Robinson had delivered the opening lecture in Peking.

Fox also went with the group to visit Saint Columban's Cathedral in Hankow, built in 1936. Here he noted that a huge statue of Saint Patrick took pride of place in the cathedral. He spoke to the Chinese priest in charge, who explained that the Irish clergy had been deported in 1949 because of their hostility to the new regime, but that there was still a strong Catholic community in Hankow and that attendance at church had never at any stage been banned.

Fox kept a diary of his impressions of China during this visit. He describes feeling as though he was following in the footsteps of Marco Polo, and – perhaps rather naively, given the subsequent development of the country into a communist dictatorship – how he saw the people of China 'emerging from a dark tunnel into the sunlight' after the defeat of the warlords. He adds that 'It was a grand, thrilling adventure to see this huge land stirring from the sleep – and sometimes the nightmare – of centuries.'[9] His account made for fascinating reading. On his return to Dublin, he turned the diary entries into a book, *China Diary*, which was published by Robert Hale of London in 1959.

Meanwhile, back in Dublin, Patricia was trying to forget about the fact that she was missing her husband by going out and about as much as possible with Amy Holland. Patricia was not hugely interested in fashion, but shopping trips into the city, followed by afternoon tea in one of the big hotels, were a novelty for her, and she threw herself into them with gusto. She and Amy also went to the theatre, the cinema and the seaside, and visited friends.

In spite of this flurry of activity, Patricia still managed to have her two books written and ready for publication in 1957. Dent published *Fiona Leaps the Bonfire*, a story of fantasy and reality intermingled, illustrated by Peggy Fortnum and dedicated 'To Jack Yeats, my friend and first illustrator, and his undying companions in Tír na nÓg', and Burke brought out *Cobbler's Luck*, more tales of the inimitable fairy shoemaker, illustrated by Christopher Brooker. As well as drafting his *China Diary*, R. M. typed the manuscripts of both new books for her and, also in 1957, had published *Jim Larkin: The Rise of the Underman*, a stirring manuscript which depicted Larkin as a heroic figure whose fierce intolerance of social injustice had made him a champion of ordinary people.[10]

Fiona Leaps the Bonfire, while fairly successful in the Irish and British markets, was not one of Patricia's top sellers. It was a great disappointment to her to find that her American publishers were not interested in bringing out the book. In August 1957, Sidney Phillips of Criterion Books, New York, wrote to E. E. Gozman of Dent to say that 'Despite our admiration for Patricia Lynch's skill and sensitivity, we shall have to decline her new book *Fiona Leaps the Bonfire.* There seems to be very little market here for this kind of fantasy.'[11] This was perhaps an indication of a change in the world market for children's literature – a market in which American children were already searching for a new, more sophisticated kind of literature.

Patricia and R.M. had been working intensely on their various writing projects all through the spring and summer of 1957. That autumn, R.M. was offered the opportunity of reporting on the Venice Film Festival for the *Irish Press;* it was decided that Patricia would go along with him and that they would make a holiday of it. It had long been a dream of Patricia's to visit this romantic city: her time in Bruges, with its canals, narrow streets and waterways, had made a lasting impression on her, and Venice, so similar in many ways, fascinated her. Although it was a working trip for R.M., who had premieres to attend and people to interview, there was also plenty of time for sightseeing. Amy Holland joined them at one stage; when R.M. was busy, she and Patricia explored the city together.

As with everything she undertook, Patricia gave herself completely to the glories of Venice and was determined to miss nothing. She was now in her early sixties and quite frail physically, but her mind, intellect and curiosity were undimmed. With her friend Amy, she wandered along canal paths and over bridges, explored the narrow little streets, and climbed the steps to the great churches and palaces. She pushed her physical strength until she was utterly exhausted. In the dungeons of the Doge's Palace, the centre of power of the Venetian state, she collapsed.

The doctor who attended to her diagnosed a strained heart muscle. He said that he thought Patricia's health condition was quite serious, and she was taken back to her hotel, where the doctor came daily to administer injections and give her oxygen for her breathing. This disaster put an end to the dream holiday, although, with Patricia too ill to return home, she and R.M. had to stay on in Venice for far longer than they had anticipated. In an article entitled 'Marooned in Venice',[12] which he wrote later, telling of this experience, Fox refers to Patricia's 'Adriatic Misadventure' and describes the kindness of the hotel staff towards her. The daughter of the hotel owner, a seventeen-year-old girl called Adriana, confided to Fox that her parents – evidently influential people in Venetian society – would, if she had died, have arranged to have Patricia buried in the Island of Flowers, a place reserved for the citizens of Venice. The island gets its name from the fact that, when Venetians travel there, they bring vast quantities of flowers to place on the graves of their loved ones.

As always, Patricia's warmth had endeared her to the family, and even with the language barrier, she had become a much-loved guest in that hotel. Her Italian doctor, so attentive to her needs, was also treating Maria Callas, the opera singer, at that time. Callas had been taken ill while holidaying in a yacht off Venice; Patricia took an impish delight in the notion that she and the greatest singer in the world were sharing a doctor!

The tourist season was coming to an end in Venice, and hotels and guesthouses were closing down. The mists were rolling up along the canals, giving the city a melancholy air. Eventually, it was decided that it would be prudent to try to get Patricia back to Dublin. On 29 September 1957, when she was feeling a little stronger, she was taken in a blue ambulance barge to the airport, from where she was flown back to Dublin. There she was met by another ambulance and taken to the Bon Secours

Nursing Home in Glasnevin to recuperate. Some years later, Patricia and her husband went back to the same hotel in Venice in order to dispel the ghosts of their experiences in the city. This they succeeded in doing while, as R.M. records, 'drinking coffee and wine on the little tables with the waves slapping rhythmically against the sides of the jetty.'[13]

Patricia enjoyed being fussed over in the nursing home, but she was also now forced to recognise her physical limitations. This knowledge, however, did not slow her creative output. While she was in the nursing home, a friend, Teresa Deevy, called on her, bringing with her a souvenir Welsh doll, dressed in a black cloak, a red skirt and a high hat. Patricia records how her dreams that night transformed the Welsh lady into a wizard, and how that wizard later became the focus of the book *Brogeen and the Black Enchanter*.[14] This was published by Burke of London in 1958 and dedicated 'To Amy – in Venice'. It was illustrated once again by Christopher Brooker, who did an excellent job of capturing the mysterious character of the wizard and created a Venetian waterfront scene for the dust jacket of the book. It is interesting to note how this story, like many of Lynch's other narratives, had its origins in a dream. As is the case with many creative people, her imagination was given full rein during her sleeping hours. She also had total recall of her dreams, the contents of which could then be woven into the fabric of her stories. The story itself is one of enchantment and fantasy, where anything can – and does – happen. In it, the O'Rourke twins, friends of Brogeen, in their bid to escape from 'the Black Enchanter', travel to Paris and Venice, meeting up with all sorts of interesting and historical figures, including the explorer Marco Polo.

Patricia's other publisher, Dent, was not to be disappointed that year either. While recuperating, Patricia also wrote *The Old Black Sea Chest: A Story of Bantry Bay*. This book, with illustrations by Peggy Fortnum, was published by Dent in 1958. The story took Lynch back to her own childhood once again, and to memories of the chest which used to stand against the wall in her grandfather's house in Fair Hill in Cork. As a little girl, she had woven many tales around this chest, 'covered with black leather, fastened by big brass nails and bound with strips of metal'.[15] The children in this narrative, Sally and Milo O'Driscoll, live in an unnamed village in County Cork with their mother Nora, while their father Timothy is wandering the world seeking his fortune.

When Timothy eventually returns to his wife and children, he brings with him his sea chest, brimful of gifts and treasures, and enough money to keep his family in some style, after their years of living on the margins. 'No more pinching and scraping, no more lace-making,' he promises.[16] Things are not as they seem, however. When Timothy opens the chest, he discovers that his wallet full of money is gone! Has it been stolen? Or could it be, as Sally and Milo suspect, that Timothy has spent the money?

The story takes quite an astute look at family life where the main breadwinner is a dreamer and a wanderer. The family are swept along on waves of promises, plans and schemes for fame and fortune. Security and stability depend on the mother's budgeting skills and her ability to keep the family afloat in times of real hardship. But life's highs come from the letters, the stories, the dreams of the father, who remains a hero in the eyes of his children, regardless of how he has – or rather, has not – provided for them.

Patricia's health troubles were not yet over. Although she recovered well from her heart problem, her sight had been deteriorating for some time. She was diagnosed with cataracts. Her illness in Venice seems to have hastened the progress of the cataracts, and soon she could see hardly anything, although she continued 'blind' writing. Sometimes her biro ran dry and she continued writing for pages and pages, while nothing appeared on the page. R.M., who was always at her side in difficult times, would often have to decipher faint lettering on the table tops where Patricia had been writing, and piece them into the sheets of paper on which her stories were scribbled, so that he could type them up for her and send the finished manuscript to the publisher. In April 1959, she was operated on for her cataracts. The operation was a great success, and she made a complete recovery: she was soon, in her own words, 'seeing the world with new eyes'.

Even while she was in hospital, with her eyes heavily bandaged, and probably in a certain amount of pain, Patricia made sure that she had a thick exercise book on the bed beside her, to jot down any ideas for stories that came to mind. And indeed, the spell in hospital was very productive in terms of her writing. In an interview in the magazine *Books and Bookmen* in December 1959, she tells how, though blind, she managed to write three books. These were *The Stone House at Kilgobbin, Jinny the Changeling* and *The Runaways*. 'One can have vision without sight,' she stated in this interview, 'and I wrote these three books without seeing a word.'[17]

More adventures of the little shoemaker Brogeen were related in *The Stone House at Kilgobbin*, which was published by Burke in 1959, with illustrations again by Christopher Brooker. She used a different publisher, Blackwell Publishing of Oxford, for *The Runaways*, also published in 1959, and in the same year Dent published *Jinny the Changeling*, with illustrations by Peggy Fortnum.

Jinny the Changeling tackled one of the major issues of the time, but in a most unusual way. Emigration was never far from Patricia Lynch's mind. It had been a feature of her childhood in Cork, where whole families had moved to England or America, and where taking the boat to start a new life abroad was part of her own experience. Being an immigrant herself in England gave her a deep insight into the hardships and joys of families that were separated from loved ones and taking on the challenge of forging a new life amidst an alien culture. Such family dislocation is the theme of *Jinny the Changeling*.

Conn Clery is a seasonal emigrant who, along with some other men from their rural community around Lough Erne, has just left on the boat to take up harvesting work in Scotland. Mrs Clery now faces the prospect of lean and lonely months, when she will have the responsibility of bringing up their children without a husband's support.

The seasonal workers of the 1940s and 1950s in effect led two lives: long months of farm work, fruit-picking, factory labour or road-building in Britain, living in hostels or cheap bed and breakfasts, lonely evenings, from which they sought solace with their friends in alcohol. The strongest and most prudent saved every penny they could, focused on a dream of one day returning to Ireland with enough money to buy a little bit of land and have their own place, where their families could live in comfort. The improvident drank their wages as soon as they got them, and their families back in Ireland had little or no income to maintain the family home. Sometimes these seasonal workers stopped communicating with their families altogether and simply never returned, leaving their wives back in Ireland in a kind of limbo, in which they had neither the support of marriage nor the dignity of widowhood. No one was more aware of the situation than Patricia, with her years spent working with the Irish community in London.

In *Jinny the Changeling,* Lynch uses her familiar structure of loss, separation, quest and eventual happiness. Mrs Clery and her children, returning home to their cottage, depressed and downhearted, having said goodbye to Conn, find a baby in the bulrushes. They rescue the baby, and discover that they have a 'changeling' – traditionally, a baby left by the fairies in exchange for a human child which they have stolen – on their hands. Having this fairy child in their midst leads to all sorts of bewildering changes in the lives of the Clery family.

A notable feature of *Jinny the Changeling,* which is part fairy tale and part adventure story, is the resourcefulness and neighbourliness of the women in this culture of absent men. When the promised money fails to materialise from Conn, the other women in the community rally around and see to it that the Clerys want for nothing. Jinny, in spite of being called 'a tinker's brat' by some of the villagers, is accepted and cherished as any child would be, and is lavishly loved by Mrs Clery and her children. What might have been a dreary, lonely life for the Clerys turns out to be anything but, and the mixture of magic, myth, folk tale and reality which Lynch brings to the narrative makes for a fascinating and exuberant tale. The story ends with Jinny returning to her own people, having brought good luck to the Clery family and having assured the young Kathy Clery that they would 'meet again in dreams'.[18]

Finishing off the 1950s with another three books to her credit was no mean achievement for Patricia. She had coped with being separated from R.M. during his visit to China, she had recovered from her heart trouble, and she had endured temporary blindness, operations and the eventual recovery of her sight – all without her creative output slowing down.

16

The Later Fiction

Patricia Lynch's sense of exile seems to have haunted her all her life. It was almost as though, in spite of the stability that R. M. Fox had provided her, she was constantly searching for an elusive place called home.

In her first book of the new decade, *Sally from Cork,* published by Dent in 1960 and illustrated by Elizabeth Grant, she is back once more in the city which shaped her both imaginatively and culturally. The protagonist here is a mirror image of Patricia Lynch herself. Sally Nolan lives in a tall old house at the bottom of Wise's Hill in Cork, a Cork which is a mixture of the rural and the urban, of the old and of the new, where 'herds of cows trotted by; men and women swarmed out of shops and offices; children ran, hopped, sauntered and gathered about the apple-women who were packing up their half-empty baskets.'[1] From her house, Sally can see the River Lee flowing down below her on its way to the great harbour, steamships starting on their voyages, and loaded lorries thundering across Patrick's Bridge. Sally's life changes dramatically when her older sister and brother arrive back from England to take her with them into exile.

Sally leaves Cork tearfully, yet with a sense of anticipation at the adventure ahead: the big ship steaming down past Blackrock Castle, having breakfast in her bunk the next morning, the clamour and clatter aboard, and the thrill of sailing past the Tower of London and disembarking in a strange city.

Sally views the prospect of settling down in London with

mixed feelings – as Patricia herself did. Sally becon
Irish diaspora in that great city; mixing with her
new community, she reflects that 'They are like all
they dream of the day when they will return. Yet w~~~~ ~~~
comes, they find it hard to go. New friends, new ambitions, a
new way of life. All this makes it difficult. But they are still
strangers in a strange land.'[2] This is a profound summing-up of
the life of the emigrant: always looking back, never quite fitting
in, yet reluctant to leave the better lifestyle and improved financial status which being in this new land offers. As she got older,
Patricia Lynch reflected more and more on the emotions and
experiences of her youth; with this reflection came a deep sympathy for those who were displaced or who felt lonely or alienat-
ed for whatever reason. *Sally from Cork* is probably the most autobiographical of Patricia's novels.

In 1960, Burke published *The Lost Fisherman of Carrigmor: A
Brogeen Story,* illustrated by Christopher Brooker. This narrative
also deals with emigration and exile, with Dinny Kelly's Aunt
Marcella returning from America to Cobh, and the family mak-
ing the trip from their home in Carrigmor to meet her. The Black
Enchanter turns up again in this story, crossing swords with
Brogeen and his pet elephant, Trud. At the end of the story, Joe
Kelly, the lost fisherman of the title, is rescued and returns
home, declaring: 'I'm sorry for anyone that hasn't a home.
Knocking around the world is all right for a while, but there
always comes a time when we need our own place and our own
people.'[3] This longing for home, a strong feature of almost all
Lynch's stories, becomes even more pronounced in her later
work. The story had its share of fantasy but was also firmly rooted in the reality of family ties and the importance of place to a
person's sense of self.

This theme of exile and the search for home continues to
surface in the books which Patricia wrote over the next few
years. In 1961, Dent published *Ryan's Fort* – illustrated by
Elizabeth Grant – which was again a mixture of legend and
adventure and dealt with the search for love and stability. Burke

published *The Longest Way Round* in 1961, illustrated by D. G. Valentine. This tells the tale of Grannie Stack, who yearns to return to her birthplace in Kerry and takes her granddaughter Nessa with her on a nostalgic journey to the place where she grew up. They travel back in time – with some help, of course, from Brogeen, the elephant Trud and the Black Enchanter.

In 1962, Dent brought out *The Golden Caddy*, illustrated by Juliette Palmer. This tells the story of the Fitzgerald children, orphaned when their father is killed in a horse-riding accident, and of their trials and tribulations as they are farmed out to various relatives. For them, exile is being separated from one another: their loss is reminiscent of Patricia's own, when she was separated from her mother and brother and had to adapt to life in other people's homes. There is a poignant moment in *The Golden Caddy* when two of the Fitzgerald children discuss what is to happen to them. Dina, trying to keep back her sobs, wipes her eyes with the back of her hand:

> 'Daddy would be ashamed of me,' she exclaims. 'I'll try not to cry again. It's so hard to be brave.'
> 'I'm just as bad as you are,' confesses her brother Gerry. 'Only I'm crying inside.'[4]

Patricia herself had done her share of 'crying inside' as a child, but she had put a brave face on her situation and had drawn solace from living in her imagination. 'I often felt very lonely and driven in on myself when I was left at a new, strange school,' she remembers. 'Then I would dream about Ireland and think of its people, its hills and valleys. These dreams would centre on Cork.'[5] A poem in her handwriting found by the current author amongst Lynch's papers epitomises this longing for family and togetherness which was such an integral part of her young life:

> The woman with the bellows blows the fire
> The flames jump up; the blackened kettle sings:
> The children on the settle watch the door,
> And chatter of the gifts their father brings.

146

There are pictures in the steam and in the fire
Far better than the pictures on the wall;
But the weary man who opens wide the door,
Sees the picture that he thinks the best of all.[6]

Never having known her own father evidently had a profound effect on the child Patricia. Her mental images of him were shaped by the stories that had been told to her by her mother and her aunts and uncles in the house in Fair Hill. Patricia lived in anticipation of the time when he would return from Egypt to be reunited with his family: then, like the families in the stories (her own and other people's), they would all be together and live, as they saying goes, happily ever after.

Burke published another of Patricia's Brogeen stories in 1962: *Brogeen and the Little Wind.* The plot for this story came about as a result of a visit Patricia made to Scotland. Following a review of *Sally from Cork* by Marion Lockhead in the *Scotsman* newspaper, Patricia was invited by Ms Lockhead to visit Edinburgh and write about Scotland in the same vivid way as she had written about London, Dublin and Cork.

Patricia, who had fond memories of the time she had spent in Scotland as a young girl, took her up on her invitation. She was the guest of the novelist Jean Matheson – whose best-known work was *The Island,* published by Collins of London in 1952 – and stayed in her apartment overlooking Edinburgh Castle. *Brogeen and the Little Wind* was based on that experience. The book was delightfully illustrated by Beryl Sanders, an illustrator whom Burke used for many of their children's books and who was to illustrate two further Brogeen books, *Brogeen and the Red Fez* – published in 1963, and inspired by a red fez which Patricia discovered and which had belonged to her father when he was living in Egypt – and *Guests at the Beech Tree,* published in 1964, and relating the tale of Brogeen doing a spot of entertaining, with dubious results.

There were no more Brogeen books after 1964, but the tales

of the little leprechaun continued to be popular in France, Germany, Austria and America, as well as in Ireland. These stories carried over well into other languages: children everywhere could identify with the mischievous characters of Brogeen and his friend Trud and had no difficulty entering the fantasy world inhabited by these characters.

Throughout the 1960s, R. M. Fox continued to keep an eye on his wife's business affairs. In one letter to W. G. Taylor, director of Dent and Sons, he stressed that 'My own over-riding consideration is to protect Patricia's position as an established and successful children's writer.'[7] He had also earlier approached Eleanor Graham, who at the time was an editor with Methuen and Co., with a suggestion for a book on Patricia's adult life. This proposal never came to anything, however: Graham wrote back to say that 'There may not be sufficient interest anywhere in children's books and their writers.'[8]

Financially, Patricia and R.M. were now more or less secure, although wealth for its own sake could never be said to have appealed to either of them. As long as they had enough on which to live in their frugal manner, and to enable them to travel when they got restless, they were content. On 8 December 1963, Patricia gave an interview to Fergus Wright of the *Sunday Independent* in which she was asked if her writing had brought her wealth as well as fame. She replied modestly: 'You could say that I have done well out of my books. They are steady sellers in many countries, and my publishers want more and more from me. I wish I was a better writer.' Patricia always derived great pleasure from the fact that she could earn her living doing the thing she most loved: writing.

R.M. and Patricia did much travelling, both within Ireland and abroad. One of their favourite places was Achill on the west coast. Along with Cork, Patricia considered this to be her spiritual home. Achill appealed to her because it was so typically Irish, encapsulating the romantic rural land of the Celtic revival. Indeed, many writers and artists have found the peace and beauty of the island conducive to their art. The great landscape artist Paul Henry visited Achill in 1910 and captured the shape and the colour of the land, the bogs and the skies in a strikingly beautiful and instantly recognisable way. Henry had studied under Whistler in Paris and, like so many others, was very much influenced by the writings of Synge, which encouraged him to return to Ireland. Henry and his wife Grace, also a gifted artist, lived and worked on Achill for many years. Their work, however, was not always appreciated by the local residents, who found Henry's landscapes a bit too modern-looking for their liking.

In an unpublished article entitled 'Hazards of a Writer', Patricia wrote: 'In Achill I stayed in a place where Paul Henry used to paint. Mrs Barrett, my landlady, was his housekeeper. When he left he gave her twelve paintings which she used to roof the henhouse. Later she opened a hotel where she had a Grace Henry painting, but she could never afford a Paul Henry.'[9] The mind boggles at the thought of those island fowl nesting beneath the work of one of Ireland's most esteemed artists. This story, exaggerated or otherwise, certainly appealed to Patricia Lynch's sense of the ridiculous.

Among the many things which Patricia loved about Achill were the aura of timelessness of the island, and the strong smell of turf which hung in the air from the sweeping blackness of the bogs, and from the smoke which curled its way upwards from the chimneys of the cottages dotted around the island. 'To see men cutting turf I prefer to go right away to Achill Island in the West – the next parish to America – where the turf is black and hard,' she wrote. 'Here no one has any sense of time. In the evenings men will stand motionless with their backs against the low stone wall until the last glimmer of daylight drains from the sky.'[10]

Other writers also found the island inspirational. Peadar O'Donnell, whom R. M. Fox greatly admired and whom he had come to know well through his work as a drama critic, produced some of his most important work whilst living in Achill. The German writer Heinrich Boll, winner of the Nobel Prize for

Literature, bought a cottage – a white-washed, horseshoe-shaped building – in the village of Dugort in 1958. He retreated to Dugort to write and lived there on and off until his death in 1985. He had a deep attachment to Achill and its people. In his *Irish Journal,* Boll records that 'Nowhere in the world have I seen so many, such lovely, such natural children.'[11] Patricia would have endorsed that sentiment. She found the island children open and friendly, with a curiosity that overcame their natural shyness.

Achill's unusual cultural and religious history – in 1834, the Reverend Edward Nangle, an evangelical minister of the Church of Ireland, set up a mission church there – put a lasting stamp on the character of the village of Dugort and its surroundings. It also made for an openness to difference amongst the people which did not exist in many other parts of Ireland at that time. This attitude appealed to Patricia Lynch, and especially to R. M. Fox – a most liberal person. Patricia used to say that she and R.M. would often set off with the intention of touring the west and north-west of Ireland, but once they arrived in Achill they had no desire to go any farther. There they found all that they wanted from a holiday.

Much as they loved Achill, Patricia and R.M. still travelled to other parts of Ireland on a fairly regular basis. They loved Kerry and made many trips there, becoming good friends with the writer John B. Keane, whom Patricia regarded, along with Brian Friel, as one of Ireland's greatest playwrights. At this stage, Keane, though highly thought of by local dramatic societies, had not yet been fully recognised by the Dublin literati; Patricia and R.M., however, were among his greatest admirers.

The year 1964 was an extraordinarily productive one for Lynch. She put together a collection of short stories under the title *The Twisted Key and Other Stories*. This book, which featured illustrations by Joan Kiddell-Monroe, was published by Harrap of London. In the same year, Patricia also had her Brogeen book, *Guests at the Beech Tree,* published by Burke, and Dent brought out *Holiday at Rosquin,* illustrated by Mary Shillabeer.

Holiday at Rosquin once again probes the themes of homelessness and loneliness. The protagonist, Bernie Nagle, is orphaned and has been farmed out to the Kelly family in Dublin. The Kellys are good to Bernie, and she is not mistreated, but nonetheless it is not home, and Bernie always feels an outsider there. She then goes on holiday to Rosquin, where she meets Garry, who is confined to a wheelchair following an accident. She subsequently decides that she never wants to leave this lovely seaside town. Bernie's determination to remain in Rosquin lands her in some dangerous situations, and this makes for an unusual and perceptive story in which there is great understanding of the problems of the child who is in any way 'different'. Lynch is at the peak of her maturity as a writer at this stage. Her characterisation is flawless and her own familiarity with both rural and urban Ireland ensures an authenticity which makes her later books particularly relevant for their era.

In 1965, Patricia received what can only be called a 'fan' letter from Dora Broome, who was well known as the author of *The Fairy Tales of the Isle of Man.* As a result of this letter, Patricia, not needing too much persuasion, paid a visit to the Isle of Man to visit Broome. She was very taken with this island and its Celtic background and kept up a correspondence with Broome. Later that year, Dent published Lynch's book *Mona of the Isle,* which was based on the legends and tales of the Isle of Man. Mary Shillabeer again illustrated this book, which Patricia dedicated to Dora Broome.

Back of Beyond, published by Dent in 1966 and illustrated by Susannnah Holden, is a very modern story dealing with the subject of children adjusting to the idea of their widowed father's remarriage. Lynch offers a deft psychological insight into the troubled minds of these vulnerable children. She handles their hurt and sense of betrayal, and their ultimate acceptance of the newcomer into their lives, with acute sensitivity, while producing a fast-moving, realistic tale. Reviewers of this novel were generous in their praise of it. One wrote that 'A fairly conventional plot – children running away from their new stepmother – gains an extra dimension by being related to the tragic and beautiful story of the Children of Lir. The rounded, likeable character of the old grandmother helps too, so does the skilful way Miss Lynch knows how to linger on pleasing, ordinary things.'[12] An American reviewer hailed the novel as 'the climax of forty years of spinning yarns.'[13] Lynch dedicated this very successful book to her dear friends Eugene and Mai Lambert.

17

The End of the Road

Lynch, now in her early seventies, was being fêted at home and abroad for her achievements in the world of children's literature. Her French publishers, G. T. Rageot of Paris, had brought out translations of most of her books, right up to *Holiday at Rosquin,* which was published in translation by them in 1968. Publishers in Germany, Spain, Portugal, Holland, Sweden, Malaya (as it then was) and America had also published editions of her work. The Irish publishers Browne and Nolan had reissued her work in a special edition for schools, using Eileen Coughlan's illustrations, and teachers for the visually handicapped used the Braille edition of *The Turf-Cutter's Donkey* in special schools. BBC television put on *The Turf-Cutter's Donkey,* read by Siobhan McKenna, as part of their *Jackanory* series in 1967. The BBC also televised *The Mad O'Haras* and *The Bookshop on the Quay.*

In 1965, the International Youth Library, sponsored by Unesco, organised an exhibition of Patricia Lynch's books in Munich. In 1967, Patricia was elected a member of the Irish Academy of Letters, joining an elite membership that included W. B. Yeats (who had founded the Academy in 1932), George Bernard Shaw and George Russell. In that same year, she was invited to Belfast as guest of honour at the PEN Club.[1] Patricia and R.M. were treated with great respect at this function, which took place on Saturday 21 January. One of the other speakers at the function was the children's writer Mrs Meta Mayne Reid, who was well known for her 'Carrigmore' series of juvenile fiction and had had *The Silver Fighting Cocks* published the year before.[2] Patricia, ever ready for an outing, enjoyed her time in Belfast, although she was far too self-effacing to make much of being the guest of honour at PEN: she always maintained that the most interesting thing about a writer was the story, not the personality.

The year 1967 also saw the publication of Patricia Lynch's final book, *The Kerry Caravan,* published by Dent and Sons and with illustrations by James Hunt – the only occasion on which this illustrator was used for her work. This book was dedicated 'To Paula – The Artist'; Paula was the daughter of Eugene and Mai Lambert.

The Kerry Caravan tells the tale of two families who set out from Dublin by horse-drawn caravan to start a new life in Kerry. It is a story of adventure and exploration, with an array of lively characters and a fast-moving narrative which is most appealing. The journey in the caravan, pulled by a bony horse called Prancing Peter, comes across as being of almost mythic proportions, punctuated at regular intervals by stops for food and shelter. This journey opens up new avenues of discovery for both families and teaches them a great deal about themselves and their ability to cope in strange and sometimes frightening places, far from the comfort of street lighting and busy streets. Their mode of transport might be primitive, but there is no sense of a hankering after an idealised past in the narrative. 'Ireland is a better place to come back to than it once was'[3] says an old man they meet along the way. The book was published in September – the same month as R. M. Fox's book *Rebel Irishwomen,* which dealt with women involved in the Irish republican struggle. *Rebel Irishwomen,* which had originally been brought out in 1935 by The Talbot Press, was re-issued by The Monument Press.

Although Patricia did not publish any more books after *The Kerry Caravan,* she certainly didn't retire. She continued to write short stories for various magazines, including the *RTÉ Guide*. On 20 December 1968, this magazine published a story of hers called 'The Golden Crock', for which she was paid the princely sum of five pounds. Another story, 'The Road to the Sea', was published in the *RTÉ Guide* on 23 May 1969. These stories brought her work to a new, adult audience and inspired a renewed interest in her books. Patricia was also continually re-writing stories which had never been published, and she also began work on another children's book, which unfortunately never came to fruition. This was to have been the story of a girl whose father and brother are on an exploring expedition in Egypt and who longs to join them but is prevented from doing so until she reaches the age of sixteen. The parallels between this story and the author's own life are clear.

At this time, Patricia was writing many articles and giving interviews, including one for Cork radio for a programme called *Mid Morning*. This followed an invitation given to Patricia on 5 April 1968 by Christine Crowley, a journalist and a member of a Cork writers' circle. Ms Crowley, on issuing the invitation, wrote: 'We are delighted to hear that you and your husband are coming to Cork later this year. Perhaps you could come to tea one after-noon. We live in the country five miles from the city centre.'[4] For Patricia, any excuse was good enough to justify a trip to her beloved Cork. She and R.M. visited the Crowley home and enjoyed a very pleasant stay there. Some time later, R.M. filled out a questionnaire at Ms Crowley's request, listing the names of Patricia's books, her publishers, the number of paperback editions of her work and the various broadcasts of versions of her books on BBC and RTÉ, as well as the names of her favourite authors and playwrights.

An interview in the September–October 1969 issue of *Ireland of the Welcomes* provides an insight into Patricia's beliefs and opinions. The unnamed interviewer describes Patricia as 'a tiny old lady, rather elfin herself . . . who is the creator of an enchanted world for children of all ages.' Patricia states in the interview that 'fact and fancy help to create the magic of Ireland which was there before we came and will remain long after we have disappeared. No nation should reject its legends or folk-lore.'[5] Throughout her life, Patricia had endorsed these views, and through her life's work she was instrumental in keeping the treasures of Ireland's past fresh for a new generation of children. She felt that it was important to pass on this heritage to children – the most receptive of audiences. To quote Patricia herself: 'I like modern children. I treat them as human beings. I don't patronise them or talk down to them. I never try to repress their imaginations or drag them up by the roots to see what makes them grow.'[6]

Though she never had children herself, Patricia Lynch had a strong empathy with young people and a great understanding of what made children tick. A crucial meeting in the 1960s gave Patricia an opportunity to experience family life first-hand – and was also to alter the course of her later life. The meeting was with Eugene and Mai Lambert, the well-known puppeteers, and parents of ten children, seven boys and three girls.

R. M. Fox did a great deal of freelance work interviewing various theatre and literary celebrities. In the early 1960s, he attended a show at the Olympia Theatre, where Ireland's best-known ventriloquist and puppeteer was performing. Eugene Lambert and his ventriloquist doll, Finnegan, were extremely popular with Irish audiences, and in huge demand for variety shows and stage acts. After the show, Fox interviewed Lambert and asked him for a photograph of himself and Finnegan for publication. Eugene was happy to oblige, and when he discovered that Fox lived quite close to his own home in Finglas, he offered to drop in the photograph himself. Eugene duly arrived the following day with the photograph. R.M. brought him in to the house and introduced him to Patricia.

Eugene's father had been Sligo County Librarian and, as a result, had had access to a vast range of reading material. As a child, he had been captivated by the imaginative content of Patricia Lynch's stories and had been an avid reader of her books. They had stimulated his own vivid imagination and had encouraged his interest in Celtic mythology and legends – something which he later put to good effect in his own career. It was a great honour for him to meet Lynch in person, and he describes that first meeting in depth:

Patricia was a very slight, frail lady with a touch of a cockney accent, a twinkle in her eye and an impish sense of humour. Their house was built in 1936 and had remained a time-capsule, as nothing had been altered since the day the builder left. A small lawn in front of the house had several large conifers which slightly shaded it. Patricia's rare garden was a virtual fairy glen, with elder trees for her famous wine, bluebells, primroses and all sorts of wild flowers. She had a tiny patch which she used to cultivate while sitting on a box; barely breaking the soil with a hand-rake, she grew a small crop of strawberries and vegetables.[7]

In his personal recollections, Lambert goes on to describe the slightly musty odour of elderberries, cloves, apples – and books – which permeated the house. He notes that the couple's furniture was sparse: apart from the book-filled glass cabinets, made for Patricia by students at Kevin Street Technical College, an old oak writing desk that doubled as a dining table, two upholstered butter boxes, two small armchairs and an old chesterfield sofa were the only other pieces of furniture.

Eugene and his wife Mai struck up a deep and lasting friendship with the Foxes. They called to see them regularly, took them on outings, had them for meals in their home and, most important of all, included them in the guest list for all their children's parties. With ten children to cater for, the Lamberts had some parties – almost one a month. These were lively, rumbustious, noisy affairs, full of magic, games, food and love. Patricia found a new and exciting world here. She entered into the spirit of it all like the child which she was at heart, and the Lambert children developed a great affection for her. R.M., too, discovered a new dimension to his life. He taught the Lambert children to play chess and loved to listen to their opinions and discuss their schoolwork and lessons with them.

The Foxes came to depend more and more on the Lamberts. When their grocery supplier, Findlaters, an old Dublin firm which had operated from 1823, closed down in 1969, they were devastated. Their list had always been phoned in to Findlaters and the groceries delivered to them on a weekly basis, and the thought of having to contend with supermarkets, shopping trolleys and fast-moving checkouts filled them with terror. The Lamberts came to their rescue once again. They were already shopping for twelve; what difference would two more make? They added the Foxes' shopping list to their own, and delivered the groceries to their door. The crisis was averted.

Patricia and R.M. were the most unworldly of couples. Although Patricia always loved food, she actually ate very little, and as she got older and more frail, she spent little time on cooking and housekeeping. Once, when Patricia and R.M. were off on one of their trips, Eugene and Mai, armed with all the tools of the trade, did a thorough spring-cleaning job on No. 39 The Rise. They cleaned and polished and waxed and scrubbed, until the house was shining. When Patricia and her husband returned, they didn't even notice how clean their house was, Eugene remembers wryly!

In an interview with the current author, Eugene recalled an incident which demonstrates how, though she loved children and enjoyed their company, Patricia was hopelessly out of her depth when it came to looking after them.[8] Eugene and Mai were doing a recording together at the RTÉ studios and were stuck for a babysitter for their two youngest little boys, aged about five and six. Patricia volunteered to take charge of the children for the day. When the Lamberts returned that evening, they found the two boys fast asleep curled up on the sofa. This was rather surprising, considering the energy levels of the two youngsters. When Eugene enquired if they had been troublesome, Patricia replied that no, they had had a great day together, sampling her elderberry wine! Eugene carried the boys home, and they didn't wake up until the middle of the next day.

Patricia would also forge notes for the children when they did not have their homework up to scratch and were afraid of getting into trouble in school. Eugene and Mai did not learn of that ruse until much later, however. Patricia was like a conspirator with the children. Like many creative people, she entered their world without difficulty, and they loved the magical universe which she presented to them.

Patricia and R.M. were invited to spend the Christmas of 1969 with the Lamberts. R.M. had not been feeling very well that winter. He had been suffering from a bad bout of flu, with complications, and had become quite frail. Eugene and Mai had the two of them around to their house in Finglas, where the Lamberts were living at that time, for Christmas day. During the course of the Christmas dinner, R.M. was taken ill. He was rushed to hospital, where he lingered on until his death on 29 December. He had celebrated his seventy-eighth birthday in the November of that year. Eugene Lambert recalls that, on his deathbed, R.M. asked to speak to a priest. Devoted to Patricia in life, he perhaps needed to feel united with her also in death.

So ended the life of a good man who, from his teenage years, had dedicated his energies to the causes of social justice, workers' rights and the eradication of exploitation of whatever sort. He spoke the truth fearlessly and was at home in any company, making no distinctions of class, creed or colour. He will also always be remembered as the steadfast rock in the life of his wife Patricia Lynch, allowing her the space and security to write her books and to develop the tales which were to delight children for generations to come. R.M. sometimes sacrificed his own work to hers, but because he loved her so deeply and believed in her so much, he did this gladly. Patricia was later to write of R.M. that 'his books were successful, but writers seldom make fortunes out of propaganda literature. He was helping the movement for human freedom, and that for him was more than wealth.'[9] Fox's biographies and profiles of Larkin, Connolly, O'Casey, Louie Bennett and the women of 1916 are a lasting testament to a man who put righteous causes before his own needs or wants. He also, it should be remembered, spent three years of his life in jail rather than compromise his principles.

Patricia was shattered by the death of her husband. For almost fifty years, they had done everything together. He had been her constant companion, her best friend, her inspiration, the love of her life. A future without him seemed bleak indeed. A poignant little poem in her handwriting, found by this author amongst Lynch's papers, articulates the desolation which she felt without him and also voices the vague anxieties which she felt about the afterlife:

> There is sorrow in the world you left behind you:
> There is sorrow in that world but laughter too.
> We shared them both, now I am lonely.
> Yet I keep wondering how it is with you.[10]

On a practical level, Patricia herself was, by now, in no fit state to live alone. R.M. had done all the cooking – such as it was – and had looked after the everyday management of their lives, and Patricia had depended on him completely. Her health was poor, she was eating very little, and the house in Glasnevin was far too large for her to cope with. There was talk of finding a place in a nursing home for her, but then, once again, the Lamberts came to the rescue. Mai Lambert had been a nurse before her marriage and, having reared ten children, was confident that she could look after Patricia as well. The Lamberts held a family conference, and it was agreed that Patricia would come to live with them in the home to which they had moved in Monkstown, a beautiful large house full of character, overlooking the sea. This was the ideal solution, although it meant a great deal of extra work for Mai. Patricia soon settled in and became like another member of the large family. Eugene recalls that Patricia was quite malnourished when she first came to live with them. Her hair had become thin and fragile, and she had little energy, but after a few months with the Lamberts there was a marked improvement in her general health and well-being.[11]

Patricia spent almost three years with the Lamberts, until her death on 1 September 1972. For the first time in her life, she was a member of a large, happy family; despite the fact that she missed R.M. deeply, she revelled in being part of that circle. She related well to the children: she loved to listen to their chatter and tales of their adventures, and they were a ready-made audience for her stories. Sometimes she would go for walks along the seashore, but as she had become quite forgetful, Eugene would follow her and bring her back when she found that she had walked too far and could not face the return journey. She also kept writing and rewriting, but there were no more books, just a few short stories, and tales for the Lambert children.

There was a great swell of support for Patricia from all over Ireland and abroad following R.M.'s death. Amongst the many letters of sympathy which she received was a moving one from the actor Mícheál Mac Liammóir, who had been well acquainted with Fox. Mac Liammóir wrote to her, saying: 'How horribly empty your life must seem without dear Richard. One feels "the moment I have dreaded all my life has come, and now there is not much worse that life can do to me." I am so glad you are with such sweet friends.'[12]

Patricia certainly appreciated her 'sweet friends'; like a child, she sometimes felt like pinching herself to affirm that the Lamberts really were her family now. She began a correspondence with Eugene's mother, Eileen, and wrote to tell her that 'Mai and Eugene have taken me to live with them. They have given me a really lovely room with a big window looking out on Dublin Bay. I can sit up in bed and look across to the mountains. Not only that, but they give me my breakfast in bed, and they have brought over all my books and ranged them on a fine set of shelves. I am very lucky to have such friends. And it's all through R.M. Sometimes I forget he has left this world, and wonder when he will becoming back, just as I used to when he was away in China or equally distant parts.'[13]

The thrill Patricia felt at getting her breakfast in bed had its roots, as always, in her childhood experiences, specifically in the home of the old west Cork *seanchaí,* Mrs Hennessy. After her long and tiring journey from Fair Hill, Patricia had fallen asleep as soon as she had arrived at the Hennessy cottage. When she awoke the next morning, she had found herself lying in the settle bed with her rag doll, Poosie, beside her, and Mrs Hennessy standing over her with a tray, waiting to treat her, 'like a lady', to a feast of rich brown tea and soda bread piled high with home-made blackberry jam. She had never had breakfast in bed before, and it had seemed like the most wonderful honour that could be bestowed on her. Now, in the care of the Lamberts, she was getting breakfast in bed every day and felt very privileged that she was being treated in such a considerate way.

On 10 July 1971, Patricia again wrote to Eileen Lambert, revealing the depth of her pain at being without R.M.:

> Now I no longer have R.M. at my back I do feel desolate. When I was a young one I had a passion for [the] *Robinson Crusoe,* Alexander Selkirk type of book. I thought it must be wonderful to be wrecked and alone on a deserted island. I don't feel that way now![14]

Surrounded by the Lambert family, there was no danger of Patricia feeling cut off from the world, and in many ways she still had a great zest for life and a curiosity about the unknown which gave her the tenacity to cling on, in spite of her poor health and her grief. In her final book, *The Kerry Caravan,* the protagonists had set off by caravan on a great adventure to start a new life in Kerry. Patricia had always been fascinated by the nomadic lifestyle, and she got the chance to experience this type of adventure herself while living with the Lamberts. Eugene and Mai, together with the younger members of the family, had set off by caravan for a holiday in the south of the country. The excitement of the children at this prospect had been infectious, and Patricia had desperately wanted to be part of the adventure. Against their better judgement, Eugene and Mai had relented and agreed to take her with them. Patricia entered into the spirit of the trip with as much exuberance as any of the children, but halfway down the country she became ill and suffered a minor heart attack. She was rushed back up to Dublin, where, fortunately, she recovered fairly rapidly. The Lamberts' holiday had to be cut short, but Eugene recalls that, as soon as the children had returned home, Patricia was sitting up in bed eager to hear of their exploits, and drinking in every detail of their experiences as nomads. The children were of course delighted at the notion that they were now the storytellers while she was the audience.[15]

Patricia never lost her sense of wonder at being part of this big, loving family. She openly acknowledged her gratitude to Eugene and Mai for their kindness to her in a letter dated 'the New Year' (presumably the new year of 1972) and written from 'Front, Upstairs':

> Dear Mai and Eugene,
>
> Thank you for giving the New Year such a lovely beginning! When R.M. was dying, though I didn't realize it, for I couldn't imagine life without him, he told me that if I was in any trouble to go to the Lamberts. I did not realise that I was facing one of the biggest troubles of my life. But you have given me a new lease.
>
> God bless you.
>
> May you have many, many Happy New Years.
>
> With thanks and love,
>
> Patricia[16]

Patricia held a very special place in the hearts and emotions of the Lambert family. Eugene admits that he felt privileged and honoured that he and Mai were in a position to look after her in her final years. Their home still holds many remembrances of her life and work. There is a pencil portrait of Patricia, done by one of the Lambert children, hanging on the wall in the drawing room, the red fez which belonged to Patricia's father has pride of place on the sideboard, her collection of miniature donkeys adorns the china cabinet, and of course her books are all over the house – a fitting monument to a lady who made it her life's work to bring joy and happiness to children everywhere. She tapped in to the imaginative potential of her young readers, always holding that 'Imagination means looking deeper and seeing beyond the veil.'[17] Patricia Lynch lifted that veil for children of all ages and gave them a glimpse into a world beyond their own.

According to a copy of her death certificate, Patricia Lynch died on 5 September 1972 (the date on her gravestone is 1 September 1972) at York House Nursing Home in Dun Laoghaire, County Dublin. The cause of death is given as 'Broncho-pneumonia, other significant conditions, fracture of the pelvis.'[18]

PART THREE

THE LEGACY OF PATRICIA LYNCH

Patricia Lynch's legacy to the world of children's literature operates on many levels. One of the most important elements in this legacy was her presentation of a vast heritage of myth, folklore and legend to a generation of children. Patricia's own childhood and her familiarity with the oral storytelling tradition gave her a natural advantage when it came to exploring Ireland's mythical past. Legends, tales of heroism, ancient sagas and folk tales had been passed on in Ireland in an unbroken continuity through the traditional storytellers, the *seanchaí*, the bards and the ballad singers of old. These tales had been related to audiences who, for the most part, could neither read nor write but who had phenomenal powers of memory, finely tuned precisely because of their lack of mastery of the written word. As the old Gaelic traditions died out, much of this folklore was in danger of being lost forever, until scholars and writers began the task of collecting, collating and recording it. In the mid- and late nineteenth century, Samuel Lover, Crofton Croker, and Lady Wilde all produced collections of Irish folk tales, purporting to be true to the original oral renderings. In reality, however, the narrative voices could not be truly captured by those who were neither Gaelic nor peasants, and W. B. Yeats himself admitted that these collections had about them a touch of 'gentle Arcadian beauty'. The authentic rawness and vividness of the language had inevitably been toned down by the collectors of the tales.

In writing her stories specifically with an audience of

children in mind, Lynch used language which was colourful and immediate, and which would draw the reader intimately into the circle of the storyteller's magic. In her *Tales of Irish Enchantment*, published in 1952, she reclaimed the stories of Fionn MacCumhaill, Cú Chulainn, Deirdre and the Sons of Usna, and the Children of Lir, in a narrative style that is powerful and full of the heroic dimension of the original legends but also accessible to young readers. Take this opening paragraph from the story 'Deirdre and the Sons of Usna':

> It was a cold bitter night with a wind that tore branches from the trees, beat the grass flat and howled about Felim's gay, bright hall. The fires burned clear although the door stood open, for Cathbad, the Druid, was outside, his arms thrust inside his thick robe, his head flung back, gazing at the stars.[1]

What child could resist such a visual narrative? And how much better if the story is being read aloud to the child, in true *seanchaí* style? This intimate inclusiveness is an integral part of all Lynch's storytelling, and it has enormous appeal. Tom Mullins of University College Cork, who has made a study of children's literature and of Lynch's writing in particular, notes that 'Her writing has the quality of continual drama about it which is reminiscent of the oral tradition. It is colloquial in language and social in tone, welcoming and inviting the reader to enter into her imaginative world. Her writing in that sense is essentially unliterary, catering for the eye, but also for the ear, so that her stories are ideally suited for reading aloud.'[2]

The deceptive simplicity of Lynch's narrative style should not detract from the seriousness of her life's work, which was to familiarise a new generation of children with the glories of Ireland's Golden Age and to alert them to the rich heritage of legend and mythology which was their birthright. In refashioning these old tales, Lynch played her part in keeping them fresh and exciting for children of a new era.

It was not just in books such as *Tales of Enchantment* and *Knights of God* that Patricia Lynch drew from the well of myth and folk memory. Almost all her fiction, in particular her early fiction, was enriched by the fusion of legend and folklore with the reality of ordinary life. *The Grey Goose of Kilnevin* is essentially a fairy tale in modern guise, with magic and strange happenings sitting comfortably alongside the story of the harsh life of a servant girl in Ireland of the 1930s. *The Turf-Cutter's Donkey* has Seamus and Eileen crossing the Road of Dreams, which takes them back in time to meet the legendary Fianna. The transition from the everyday life of the two children through the mists of time to a pre-Christian Ireland is made so seamlessly that it seems the most natural thing in the world. Again, in *King of the Tinkers*, Miheal, the hard-working son of a poor widow woman, sets out to seek his fortune and finds himself in a Secret Valley beneath the shadow of the steepest, strangest mountain he has ever seen. He is lost, frightened, trying to be brave, and then the narrator tells us:

> He remembered the story his mother had told him how Finn Mac Cool and the Fianna – the ancient warriors of Ireland – lived in a hidden valley until the great days of Ireland would come again. Many had set out to find it. Some never were seen again, and those who came back told how they had heard sweet music and laughter but could not discover where this came from.[3]

What follows is a tale of adventure, magic, history and myth. It makes an exciting read for children but also, almost subconsciously, alerts young minds to the richness of a heritage which would not be found in history books.

Lynch rose to the challenge of bringing the old legends and folk tales alive in her own individualistic way. The importance of maintaining the vigour of such stories should not be underestimated: the tales offer a deep insight into the nation's past and into the culture of a people, from the pagan Celts to the golden age, that made Ireland a land of learning and culture which came to be known as the 'island of saints and scholars'. Lynch brought those times to life with flair, and did so in such a way as to make the journey into the past an appealing one for children, thus stimulating their natural curiosity and inviting them to explore further.

Lynch was always quite deliberate in avoiding the depiction of menace or evil in her narratives – something which is not true of other traditional storytellers. Fairy stories which emerge from central European sources, for instance, are full of threat and menace. The gruesome violence of traditional narratives such as the story of Little Red Riding Hood – who finds herself confronted by a wolf posing as her beloved grandmother and who escapes the jaws of said wolf only when the woodcutter slashes the animal with his axe and pulls granny free from its stomach – is not found in Lynch's interpretation of Irish folklore and legend. When, in the nineteenth century, the Brothers Grimm put together their collection of folk tales and fairy stories, they produced a volume of heart-stopping terror. Who can forget the fear instilled by the plight of Hansel and Grettel wandering through the dark woods, or the sense of evil which emanated from the figure of the wolf sitting up in bed wearing the granny's bonnet? The tales were not sanitised in any way, and preserved the full impact of medieval superstition and subversive logic. Children who read these stories were left in no doubt about the evil which existed in the world and which could dog them if they stepped out of line.

Wordsworth said that the two great emotions of childhood are joy and fear, but in her *Tales of Enchantment,* as in her many other works, Patricia Lynch chose to emphasise the joy rather than the fear. The 'heart of darkness' was not a scenario which she chose to explore in her fiction. Her vision of the world is an optimistic one: although there are threats and dangers in her stories, ultimately the good outweighs the bad, and virtue triumphs over wrongdoing. And at the culmination of every narrative is the security of having a safe haven to return to. Nevertheless, she was conscious of the need for balance, and she said at one stage: 'I don't believe we should keep out of children's books mention of tragedy and suffering. Everything human (suited to the stage of their understanding) has its rightful place.'[4]

Fantasy is a powerful way of stimulating the imagination, and a vivid imagination surely adds depth to a child's life. C. S. Lewis wrote that the child 'does not despise real woods because he has read of enchanted woods: the reading makes all real woods a little enchanted.'[5] Patricia Lynch in her fiction played her part in developing this important aspect of a child's development.

In 'The Shadow Pedler', one of the wonderful short stories originally included in the collection called *The Seventh Pig,* published by Dent in 1950 – and in 1959 included in *The Black Goat of Slievemore,* also published by Dent – young Kevin Hanlon escapes from the drabness and harshness of his home surroundings by retreating into the world of fantasy and dreams. The language in this story is very evocative of rural Ireland in a time of poverty and deprivation. Kevin's job is to keep the home fires burning – an important task in a winter climate that is relentlessly wet:

> Kevin grabbed sods from the end of the pile nearest the cabin and quickly packed them in the creel. . . . The rain seeped through the sack and trickled inside his collar. Spray from the rocks below tossed up in his face, rain dripped noisily from the overhanging thatch, and the wind tried to drag away the sack he had thrown over his head and shoulders.[6]

Young though he is, Kevin is expected to play his part in the family's rural economy and to shoulder his share of the burdens. Kevin, however, is a dreamer and has the unhappy knack of messing up every job he tackles – unlike his older brother John, who is already an accomplished carpenter, and his sister Bridie, who is such an expert with her needle, she can sew dresses for her new baby sister. Kevin dreams himself away from the mists,

171

rain and hard labour into a land of sunshine, blue skies and ease. He dreams of all the gifts he will buy for his family for Christmas. He dreams of the poems he has learned in school and of the stories he has heard at home. He wishes he could be good at something, but his dreams always get in the way, and the job is left unfinished or half-done. And then Kevin meets the Shadow Pedler, who tells him that dreams are the most important thing in the world. The Pedler buys Kevin's dreams, to distribute to those who are unlucky enough not to be able to reach beyond the reality of their everyday world, and suddenly Kevin's flights of imagination become valuable assets and Kevin no longer feels a failure.

A story like 'The Shadow Pedler' validates the child's right to daydream. Dreams enrich the spirit, and children will always need to be able to switch off from their ordinary world and tune into the magical world of fantasy, to a vision beyond their own horizons, where anything is possible and the spirit can take flight. Child psychologists have long recognised the importance of imagination and fantasy to child development. In 1987, Margaret and Professor Michael Rustin, psychotherapist and sociologist respectively, who made a study of this subject, wrote that 'The capacity to maintain an internal resilience to temporarily bad experiences . . . is crucial to development, and depends in part on powers of language, play and imagination.'[7]

Patricia Lynch is sometimes accused of being stuck in a time warp and of concentrating her stories on a stagnant, rural Ireland. While much of her earlier output featured a rural background – after all, Ireland of the 1930s and 1940s was predominantly rural – she did evolve and become more outward-looking in her later fiction. Narratives like *The Bookshop on the Quay* (1956), *Sally from Cork* (1960), *Back of Beyond* (1966) and *The Kerry Caravan* (1967) reflect a more modern Ireland, an Ireland which is changing and looking outward, and whose children are being exposed to influences beyond their own locality or parish. Rural electrification, more modern modes of transport, the growth of tourism – resulting in an influx of foreign visitors – and, most of all, the advent of television made for a new, more worldly-wise breed of reader. Lynch rose to this challenge while sacrificing none of the charm and uniqueness of her earlier creative output.

Eugene Lambert notes that, although Patricia loved children, she actually had very few dealings with them after her own childhood, so exposure to his family of ten children in the 1960s gave her a fresh insight into the lifestyle of the modern child. She loved being included in the Lamberts' family outings and parties, and this undoubtedly gave her work a fresh impetus and introduced a sense of social realism which may have been lacking in some of her earlier fiction. Robert Dunbar, in his introduction to the excellent *Secret Lands: The World of Patricia Lynch,* remarks that 'for the modern reader, there is a danger that the stories' original, simple charm may now seem to be mere whimsy or sentimentality, the literary equivalent perhaps of a dated John Hinde postcard view of the Irish landscape.'[8] I believe, however, that this does not do justice to the child's ability to rise above time and place and transport him or herself into the imaginary world which unfolds on the page. In the realms of the imagination, anything can happen and there are no boundaries. I would be more inclined to agree with J. R. R. Tolkien, who believed that 'providing an alternative to reality is one of the primary properties of language'.[9]

A feature of Lynch's books which was perhaps unusual for her time was the feistiness and the strength of her female characters. The role of women in Irish folk tales and legends has always been a powerful one. Queen Maeve, for instance, in the *Táin Bó Cuailnge,* took on the armies of Ulster fearlessly in her battle for the Bull of Cooley. The pirate queen Granuaile was legendary for her courage and loyalty; with her fleet of forty ships, she protected her people in the west of Ireland from maurading invaders. On another level there was Saint Brigid, who faced the wrath of the pagan chieftains in her determination to found her convent and set up a seat of learning in Kildare.

Life had taught Patricia Lynch that self-reliance was all-important. Her nomadic childhood nurtured in her an independence of spirit and a confidence in her ability to survive, whatever life might throw at her. This confidence is reflected in her female fictional characters. Delia of *Delia Daly of Galloping Green,* Ethne Cadogan of *Fiddler's Quest,* Nuala Brophy of *Back of Beyond,* Tessa Nolan of *Tinker Boy* and Grania O'Hara of *The Mad O'Haras* are all strong, positive young women who know what they want and are not prepared to play second fiddle to their male counterparts. Compare this with, for instance, the female characters in Enid Blyton's fiction. Anne of the 'Famous Five' stories is the brake on the boys' adventures. She is the one who advises caution, slows down the boys, looks after them even when they are older than her, and sees to it that they are fed. When decisions need to be made, she defers to the males in the group because she is 'only a girl' and therefore not able to take charge. Then there is George – a very different type of female character, who gains her sense of power from aping the males. George resents being female. She dresses like a boy, cuts her hair short like a boy, and struts and fights and bosses, and so she is accepted on the same level as the male characters. Lynch's fictional girls are proud of being girls but do not in any way compromise their right to experience adventure, excitement and risk.

In *The Mad O'Haras,* Grania overcomes her fears and goes to join the cast of eccentric characters in Castle O'Hara. She is determined to follow her star and become an artist, although her 'place in the world' would dictate that she become apprenticed to a dressmaker and live out her days serving her betters. She stands her ground against the bullying of her 'mad' cousins in the crumbling castle and ignores the jibes of the local community, who despise the O'Haras because they have tinker blood in them. Grania believes in herself and in her talents; eventually, against all the odds, she realises her ambition and wins a scholarship to the College of Art in Dublin.

Ethne Cadogan of *Fiddler's Quest* makes the journey across the Irish Sea alone in search of the elusive King Cadogan, her grandfather, who is supposed to take care of her now that her father has gone to America to make his fortune. Ethne puts her fears and loneliness behind her, and makes the best of the life into which she is thrown. When there is no sign of grandfather Cadogan coming to claim her, she throws in her lot with the widow Rafferty and her five youngsters, and when money is tight she uses her talents as a fiddler to earn money to help pay for her keep. Eventually King Cadogan turns up, and together they travel to Inishcoppal, the ancestral home of the Cadogans. Ethne has earned her right to her inheritance and has proved herself worthy of her place on the island. Captain Hennessy, master of the ship which brings Ethne to Ireland, sums up the philosophy which Ethne makes her own when he says to her, as she bravely winks away her tears at being left by her father: 'A good sailor never frets for the port he's leavin'. He just thinks of the port he's bound for.'[10]

Yet another strong, independent female character is Tessa in *Tinker Boy,* who champions the young traveller, Dara MacDara, in the face of much hostility and opposition from her community. Not only does she defend his right to attend the village school, but Tessa also overcomes local prejudice and becomes friends with the MacDara family, sharing meals with them and learning of their history and culture.

In her narratives, Lynch could not be said to have questioned openly the position of women in the society of her day. By portraying her female characters in such a positive light, however, she let her young readers see that there was no reason why girls should take a back seat to boys or be inactive spectators in life's adventures. In the 1950s and 1960s, other Irish writers such as Meta Mayne Reid took up the cudgels on behalf of female heroines, but, in the reckoning of the current author, Patricia Lynch led the field in this regard.

One of the great achievement of Lynch as a writer was to introduce Irish children to books and stories in which the protagonists come from backgrounds which are grounded in the Irish landscape, rural and urban, and where the characters voice the concerns of Irish children. In this respect, she established a new literature for young Irish readers. Before Lynch, there was almost no indigenous children's literature in Ireland. In the nineteenth century, Maria Edgeworth produced some children's stories, but these were didactic, moralistic and for the most part not particularly appealing to either children or young people. A year after the publication, in 1800, of the anarchic and slyly subversive *Castle Rackrent* – which did not meet with the approval of her father and mentor Richard Lovell Edgeworth – Maria Edgeworth published *Moral Tales for Children,* which was widely read by children of a certain class in Victorian Ireland. Edith Somerville and Martin Ross also tried their hand at children's stories, with perhaps more success than Edgeworth. Somerville's 'The Story of the Discontented Little Elephant', in particular, was quite charming, but these stories could be said to have been from the outside looking in and not to have captured the cultural identity of native Irish children. In *Inventing Ireland,* Declan Kiberd reminds us that, until the Gaelic League's campaign of Gaelic revival bore fruit, schoolchildren in Irish classrooms recited the following lines at morning assembly:

Thank the goodness and the grace
That on my birth have smiled;
And made me in these Christian days
A happy English child.[11]

Such was the cultural ethos in Ireland at that time that Irish children for the most part had to turn to British writers for their literary and imaginative nourishment. This undoubtedly helped to shape young minds into believing that the British way of life was superior to their own and that more exciting things happened to British children than to Irish children, thus fostering that feeling of inferiority which colonisation inevitably produces.

To sum up, although some Irish children's authors, including Winnifred Letts, Ella Young and Janet MacNeill, reached a wide readership, children growing up in the Ireland of the 1940s and 1950s were, to a large extent, nourished on a diet of stories in which the fictional characters embraced a culture which was alien to that of their Irish readers, and with whose lives they would have found it hard to identify. Patricia Lynch provided a popular alternative for Irish children: her stories featured heroes and heroines with whom they could empathise and who had cultural backgrounds with which they could identify. This was important for various reasons. In the first place, Lynch's stories gave great pleasure to her many readers. Also, at that time, with mass emigration and poor living standards, a sense of pride in Irishness and in an Irish way of life certainly needed encouragement. The wonderfully realistic atmosphere of Patricia Lynch's stories, into which fantasy and magic are so effortlessly blended, appealed to a wide readership, and it was – and remains – a source of justifiable pride that a children's writer from Ireland should also be so highly regarded internationally.

IMAGES

Patricia Lynch's childhood was a mixture of love and neglect, of insecurity and anxiety. But it was also rich in imaginative stimulation and full of exciting experiences which would, in time, feed into her creative potential. Her early years – the years during which the groundwork for one's adult life is prepared – were spent in an atmosphere imbued with learning. Through local storytellers and especially through the *seanchaí* Mrs Hennessy, she was enveloped in a powerful oral culture which drew on elements of myth, fantasy and folklore. Through her grandfather, who spent years writing a history of the Irish nation in Gaelic, she developed a strong interest in Ireland's past and in the struggles and sufferings which shaped the nation. From him too she developed a deep love of reading and of the written word. Through her father – a man whom she never got to know – she inherited a yearning for travel and excitement, for seeing new places and experiencing different cultures and different ways of living. Her mother instilled in her a love of family and a respect for other people's ways, and she also nurtured in her a sense of yearning for the unattainable, and that intense longing for something beyond the horizon which became an integral part of Patricia's character.

Patricia was also fortunate to have been born with a happy disposition. Although it could be argued endlessly whether nurture or nature was the stronger in making her who she was, there is no doubt that she made the best of life's difficulties and inevitably saw the good rather than the bad in other people.

Patricia remained childlike and open to the end of her days. Eugene and Mai Lambert felt privileged to have shared their home with her in her final years, and even then, with her health poor, her body frail, and her heart grieving for her late husband, she remained alert and interested, and eager to join in any new adventure or excitement which the young Lamberts could provide.

Patricia Lynch's stories opened up a new world of wonder for Irish children in an era of drabness, insularity and economic stagnation. I have a strong recollection of sitting on the floor in front of the big turf fire at home, my father rattling the newspaper in the background, my mother reading to me in her soft storyteller's voice. I am lost in the world of the grey goose Betsy, of Sheila, of the cruel Big Maggie. I long for Sheila to find kindness from someone. I want to see Big Maggie punished for her meanness. I know that there is magic in the world, and I see nothing strange in a talking goose. When my mother reads *The Turf-Cutter's Donkey* to me, I ache to own a donkey like Long Ears, and I dream of the day when I will be old enough to have adventures like Eileen and Seamus.

As soon as I had mastered the art of reading, I would, oblivious to the world around me, immerse myself in the adventures of Miheal in *King of the Tinkers*, of Grania in *The Mad O'Haras*, of Ethne in *Fiddler's Quest*. Of course I was also at that stage reading and enjoying Enis Blyton's stories, Richmal Crompton's 'Just William' books, Grimms' *Fairy Tales*, Robert Louis Stevenson's *Treasure Island*, as well as *The Beano*, *The Dandy* and *Film Fun*, and the strange tales of *The Arabian Nights*. The works of Patricia Lynch had a special immediacy for me, however. Her stories were set in backgrounds with which I could identify. I had travelled that bog road with my father. I had walked that mountain path with my mother. I had played in a fairy rath with my friends and felt the thrill of fear as we entered that mysterious place. The characters who peopled her books were my neighbours, my companions at school, the workers on my uncle's farm, the maids who 'did' for us at home, the shop-keeper who sold us our bull's eyes, Peggy's legs and aniseed balls.

The noise and excitement of the fair days, so brilliantly depicted in Patricia Lynch's narratives, were central to my life too. The fairground also came to my town. I knew what it was like to save up my pennies, hording them in the purse which I had knitted myself, and, like Nora in *King of the Tinkers,* I knew the exquisite dilemma of trying to decide between the swing-boats, the wheel of fortune and the sweet stall. Having made my choice, I could, like Nora, experience the churning in my stom-ach and the wind in my ears as the swingboat soared higher and higher, and the people in the fairground seemed like dolls on the ground below:

> Nora and Jerry pulled together and up flew the boat. Nora had never been in a swing before. As they rose and they saw the Fair Ground with its crowds and stalls and the grey horse rearing up all beneath her, she was terri-fied. She wanted to scream – 'Let me out! Let me get out!' But she was ashamed and, without saying a word, closed her eyes. When she opened them again she was afraid no longer.[1]

I could identify with Nora, just as I could identify with the characters in Patricia Lynch's other books. And I know that my experience was not unique. Her stories were an integral part of so many Irish children's lives. They held a special place in Irish culture, both shaping and reflecting the country's cultural identi-ty. Certainly my childhood was enriched by the fiction of my favourite writer. Her lyrical use of language gave me a feeling for words which has been a joy to me throughout my life. Her story-teller's voice conjured up wondrous new worlds, and her casual acceptance of the strange and the magical opened my young eyes to the rich enchantment of life and of living.

But what of today's children? It is almost forty years since the publication of Patricia Lynch's final book, *The Kerry Caravan,* and in that time children's lives, needs and expectations have changed enormously. There is now, in Ireland, a flourishing indigenous publishing industry and a substantial market for children's books written by Irish authors. Books of high literary quality written by Irish authors, illustrated by Irish artists and – at least some of the time – published by Irish publishing firms are now the norm rather than the exception. The market has never been so well served. So, have children's tastes and expectations changed over the years? In spite of the more complicated lifestyles of today's youngsters, and of their increased sophistication, there is no evidence that they have lost their sense of wonder. They still demand much the same ingredients from a story as their parents and grandparents did. They still need to be hooked by a gripping plot. They still need to be able to identify with the characters and with the worlds which these characters inhabit. And, most of all, they still need to stretch their imaginative powers and lose themselves in fantasy, magic and adventure. Consequently, I believe that the lively and endearing characters which were the product of Patricia Lynch's imagination will always find a place in children's hearts.

In conclusion, I should like to reiterate the sentiments of Howard Pyle, the much-esteemed American author, illustrator and children's writer. Pyle surely voiced the sentiments of all who love reading when he wrote that 'In one's mature years, one forgets the books that one reads, but the stories of childhood leave an indelible impression.'[2] This indelible impression is, I believe, one of Patricia Lynch's great gifts to the world of children's literature.

NOTES

PART ONE

1 THE BACKGROUND

1 Robert Gibbings, *Lovely is the Lee* (London: Dent, 1945) p. 121
2 Edmund Spenser, quoted in Gibbings, ibid., p. 121
3 Patricia Lynch, *A Storyteller's Childhood* (London: Dent, 1947) p. 16
4 Ibid., p. 5
5 Ibid., p. 4
6 Ibid., p. 2
7 Ibid., p. 4
8 Ibid., p. 10
9 Ibid., p. 9

2 THE WANDERING YEARS

1 R. F. Foster, *Modern Ireland, 1600–1972* (London: Penguin, 1989) p. 356.
2 Lynch, op. cit., p. 7
3 Ibid., p. 11
4 Ibid., p. 14
5 Ibid., p. 15
6 Ibid., p. 21
7 Ibid., p. 24
8 Ibid., p. 26
9 Robert Dunbar, *Secret Lands: The World of Patricia Lynch* (Dublin: O'Brien Press, 1998), p. 19
10 Lynch, op. cit., p. 34
11 Ibid., p. 61
12 Ibid., p. 83
13 Ibid., p. 90
14 Gibbings, *Sweet Cork of Thee* (New York: Dutton, 1951) p. 55

3 EMIGRANTS

1 Lynch, op. cit., p. 125
2 Ibid., p. 126
3 Ibid., p. 139
4 Ibid., p. 154

4 SCHOOLDAYS

1 Lynch, op. cit., p. 197
2 Ibid., p. 217
3 Ibid., p. 277
4 Ibid., p. 300
5 Ibid., p. 307
6 Ibid., p. 310
7 Ibid., p. 314
8 Ibid., p. 321

5 GOODBYE TO CHILDHOOD

1 Lynch, op. cit., p. 332
2 Ibid., p. 341

6 MOVING ON

1 *Chronicle of the 20th Century* (London: Chronicle Communications Ltd., 1988) p. 112
2 Lynch, *Irish Press,* 1957; interview conducted by Julia Monks
3 Foster, op. cit., p. 436–44
4 Lynch, *Irish Press* article dated 17 February 1936

7 GETTING THE NEWS ACROSS

1 *Freeman's Journal,* 5 May 1916, quoted in J. C. Beckett, *The Making of Modern Ireland 1603–1923* (London: Faber and Faber, 1966), p.441.
2 Lynch article 'Scenes from the Rebellion' from a pamphlet entitled *Rebel Ireland* (London: The Workers' Socialist Federation, undated).
3 Letter from Maud Gonne to Patricia Lynch, undated. National Library of Ireland, Collection List No. 79: Papers of Patricia Lynch and R. M. Fox. MS 40, 327/9.
4 Lynch, 'Memories of Countess Markievicz', *Irish Press,* 19 September 1968.
5 Lynch, 'A Timely Thought', *An Phoblacht,* 19 March 1932. National Library of Ireland, Collection List No. 79: Papers of Patricia Lynch

and R. M. Fox (MS 40, 308/2).

6 Lynch, untitled article in *Daily Independent,* 23 July 1920. National Library of Ireland, Collection List No. 79: Papers of Patricia Lynch and R. M. Fox (MS 40, 308/2).

8 GETTING STARTED

1 Lynch, 'E. Nesbit, A Victorian Spellbinder', *Puffin Post,* Vol. 1, No. 3, autumn 1967, pp. 4–5. National Library of Ireland, Collection List No. 79: Papers of Patricia Lynch and R. M. Fox (MS 40,308/2).

2 Lynch, 'A Storyteller Grows Up', unpublished MS, dated 1 December 1971, p. 54. National Library of Ireland, Collection List No. 79: Papers of Patricia Lynch and R. M. Fox (MS 40, 290/1)

3 Ibid., p. 55

9 R. M. FOX

1 Lynch, 'A Storyteller Grows Up', unpublished MS, dated 1 December 1971, p. 62. National Library of Ireland, Collection List No. 79: Papers of Patricia Lynch and R. M. Fox (MS 40, 290/1)

2 Ibid, p. 69

3 *Irish Digest,* Dublin, May 1953

4 R. M. Fox, ed., *The Rebel* Vol. l, No. 1., Oct. 1916. (Collaborators P. Howard and W. Savage).

5 References to this landlady, a Mrs O'Dwyer, can be found in 'A Storyteller Grows Up', unpublished MS, dated 1 December 1971. National Library of Ireland, Collection List No. 79: Papers of Patricia Lynch and R. M. Fox (MS 40, 290/1)

6 Lynch, 'A Storyteller Grows Up', unpublished MS, dated 1 December 1971, p. 67. National Library of Ireland, Collection List No. 79: Papers of Patricia Lynch and R. M. Fox (MS 40, 290/1)

7 Ibid., p.67

8 Letter from R. M Fox to Patricia Lynch, dated 1 June 1922. National Library of Ireland, Collection List No. 79: Papers of Patricia Lynch and R. M. Fox (MS 40, 327/4)

9 Letter from R. M Fox to Patricia Lynch, dated 4 July 1922. National Library of Ireland, Collection List No. 79: Papers of Patricia Lynch and R. M. Fox. (MS 40, 327/4)

10 Fox, handwritten notes (undated). National Library of Ireland, Collection List No. 79: Papers of Patricia Lynch and R. M. Fox. (MS 40, 355/1-2).

1 Fox, 'Present Day Berlin: An Impression', the *Wheatsheaf,* April 1923, p. 51. National Library of Ireland, Collection List No. 79: Papers of Patricia Lynch and R. M. Fox (MS 40, 388/3)

2 Frank O'Connor 'Æ – A Portrait' from *The Best of the Bell,* ed. Seán McMahon (Dublin: O'Brien Press, 1978) p. 18

3 *Irish Statesman,* Dublin, 3 November 1923

4 Letter and notes for preface from Æ to Fox, dated 7 September 1929. National Library of Ireland, Collection List No. 79: Papers of Patricia Lynch and R. M. Fox. (MS 40, 327/12)

5 Ibid.

6 Fox, 'Æ: A Voice in Irish Democracy', *Progress Monthly,* 1944 (no month given), p. 40. National Library of Ireland, Collection List No. 79: Papers of Patricia Lynch and R. M. Fox. (MS 40, 372/2)

7 E. Nesbit article published in the *Christian Commonwealth,* 27 February 1918

PART TWO

11 THE WRITER IS BORN

1 Lynch, 'A Storyteller Grows Up', unpublished MS, dated 1 December 1971, p. 68. National Library of Ireland, Collection List No. 79: Papers of Patricia Lynch and R. M. Fox (MS 40, 290/1)

2 Lynch, 'Children and Imagination', unpublished and undated MS, p. 1. National Library of Ireland, Collection List No. 79: Papers of Patricia Lynch and R. M. Fox. (MS 40, 308/2)

3 Unnumbered file in Munster Literature Centre, Cork

4 Theo Snoddy, ed., *Dictionary of Irish Artists, 20th Century* (Dublin: Wolfhound Press, 1996)

5 Lynch, *The Turf-Cutter's Donkey* (London: Dent & Sons, 1934), p. 245

6 Jack Yeats quoted in *The Lion and the Unicorn,* Vol. 21, No. 3, September 1997

7 Unnumbered File in Munster Literature Centre, Cork

8 Ibid.

9 Letter in Dent correspondence file from E. P. Dutton and Co. Publishers, New York, dated 27 October 1938 to Patricia Lynch

10 Patricia Lynch, *King of the Tinkers* (London: Dent, 1938), pp. 95–6

11 Letter in Dent file from Patricia Lynch, dated 3 November 1947

12 Quote from unpublished lecture delivered by Tom Mullins of UCC on

19 December 1998. Given to the author by Dr Mullins, February 2002

13 Lynch, *The Grey Goose of Kilnevin* (London: Dent, 1939), p. 214

14 Ibid., p. 279

15 David Norris and Roy Foster, quoted in 'Education and Living', the *Irish Times,* 8 December 1998

16 'Writing for Children', *Journal of the National Book League,* No. 302, June 1956.

12 LIFE IN THE 1940s

1 Lynch, *Fiddler's Quest* (Dublin: Poolbeg, 1994), p. 100

2 Ibid., p. 102

3 Letter in Dent File, dated 24 October 1947

4 Joan Kiddell-Monroe, letter to Patricia Lynch, dated 2 September 1943. National Library of Ireland, Collection List No. 79: Papers of Patricia Lynch and R. M. Fox. (MS 40, 327/8)

5 Letter in Dent file, dated 24 October 1947

6 Samuel Taylor Coleridge, quoted in 'The Adventures of a Donkey' (London: Norman-Stahli Publication, 1971), p. 1

7 J. M. Synge, *Collected Works II: Prose* (Bucks., UK: Colin Smythe, 1982) p. 163.

8 E. Somerville & V. M. Ross, *The Silver Fox* (London: Lawrence & Bullen Ltd., 1898)

9 Lynch, *The Turf-Cutter's Donkey,* p. 4.

10 Lynch, untitled article in *The Cross* (Passionist Fathers' magazine), May 1942

11 Lynch, *The Grey Goose of Kilnevin,* p. 45.

12 See Jullia Eccleshare, *Beatrix Potter to Harry Potter: Portraits of Children's Writers* (London: National Portrait Gallery Publications, 2002)

13 *Journal of the SPCA* (quote from the Dalai Lama)

13 THE WAR YEARS

1 Letter dated 22 February 1943, Dent file

2 Internet site *www.catholicauthors.com/lynch.html*

3 Letter dated 31 December 1946 from Eleanor Graham, 17 Queen Court, Queen Square, WC1, Munster Literature File

4 Lynch, *Brogeen of the Stepping Stones* (London: Kerr-Cross Publishing Co., 1947), p. 9

5 Internet site *www.catholicauthors.com/lynch.html*

6 Letter from Browne and Nolan to Dent, dated 18 December 1947, Dent file

7 Undated letter, Dent file

8   Lynch, *The Mad O'Haras* (Dublin: Poolbeg, 1997), p. 65.
9   Jeanne Cappe, *Littérature de Jeunesse,* September 1954
10 Teresa Deevy National Library of Ireland Collection List No. 79: Papers of Patricia Lynch and R. M. Fox (MS 40, 312/1)

14 Two Books a Year

1   Letter dated 10 June 1950, Dent file
2   Peggy Fortnum, *Running Wild* (London: Chatto and Windus, 1975)
3   Lynch, *Brogeen and the Green Shoes* (Dublin: Poolbeg, 1989), p. 209
4   Letter dated 11 November 1953, Dent file
5   Lynch, *Tinker Boy* (London: Dent, 1955) p. 15
6   Ibid., p. 181
7   Lynch, *The Bookshop on the Quay* (London: Dent, 1956) p. 12
8   Ibid., p. 184
9   Ibid., p. 186

15 Living and Writing

1   Christine Crowley, *Eirigh, A Magazine of Christian Optimism,* January 1970
2   Interview in *Model Housekeeping* magazine, December 1954. National Library of Ireland Collection List No. 79 : Papers of Patricia Lynch and R. M. Fox (MS40, 312/2)
3   Letter from Franz Fromme to R. M. Fox, dated 6 June 1956. National Library of Ireland, Collection List No. 79: Papers of Patricia Lynch and R. M. Fox. (MS 40, 327/6)
4   Letter from Patricia Lynch to Christine Crowley, dated 2 April 1968, Munster Literature Centre File
5   Lynch, 'A Storyteller Grows Up', p. 2. National Library of Ireland, Collection List No. 79: Papers of Patricia Lynch and R. M. Fox (MS 40, 290/1)
6   Lynch, 'Ireland of the Young', unpublished article, p. 3. National Library of Ireland, Collection List No. 79: Papers of Patricia Lynch and R. M. Fox (MS 40, 308/1)
7   Jane Healy, profile of Patricia Lynch, undated. National Library of Ireland, Collection List No. 79: Papers of Patricia Lynch and R. M. Fox. (MS 40, 312/4)
8   Letter from Amy Holland to R. M Fox, dated 20 September 1956. National Library of Ireland, Collection List No. 79: Papers of Patricia Lynch and R. M. Fox. (MS 40, 327/7)
9   Fox, *China Diary* (London: Robert Hale, 1959), p. 184.

10 Fox, *Jim Larkin: The Rise of the Underman* (London: Lawrence and Wishart, 1957)

11 Letter from Sidney Phillips to E. E. Gozman, dated August 1957, Dent file.

12 Fox, 'Marooned in Venice', *Irish Independent,* 8 August 1967

13 Ibid.

14 Lynch, 'Hazards of a Writer', unpublished, undated MS. National Library of Ireland, Collection List No. 79: Papers of Patricia Lynch and R. M. Fox. (MS 40, 308/1)

15 Lynch, *A Storyteller's Childhood,* p. 4.

16 Lynch, *The Old Black Sea Chest* (London: Dent, 1958), p. 24.

17 'Interview with Patricia Lynch', *Books and Bookman,* December 1959

18 Lynch, *Jinny the Changeling* (London: Dent, 1959), p. 171

16 THE LATER FICTION

1 Lynch, *Sally from Cork* (London: Dent, 1960), p. 1

2 Ibid., p. 173

3 Lynch, *The Lost Fisherman of Carrigmor* (London: Burke, 1960), p. 98

4 Lynch, *The Golden Caddy* (London: Dent, 1962), p. 12

5 Internet site *www.catholicauthors.com/lynch.html*

6 Lynch, 'Coming Home', undated, unpublished poem. National Library of Ireland, Collection List No. 79: Papers of Patricia Lynch and R. M. Fox. (MS 40, 307/2)

7 Letter from R. M. Fox to W. G. Taylor, dated 30 November 1960. Dent file

8 Letter from Eleanor Graham to R. M. Fox, dated 1955. Dent file.

9 Lynch, 'Ireland: The Country of the Young', unpublished, undated ms, p. 5. National Library of Ireland, Collection List No. 79: Papers of Patricia Lynch and R. M. Fox. (MS 40, 308/1)

10 Lynch, 'My Ireland', *Ireland of the Welcomes,* September–October 1969, Vol. 18, No. 3

11 Heinrich Boll, *Irish Journal* (New York: McGraw-Hill, 1971)

12 *Times Literary Supplement,* 25 May 1966

13 *Tamalpa Times,* 4 May 1966

17 THE END OF THE ROAD

1 Details of the PEN award are recorded in the *Belfast Newsletter,* 16 January 1967. National Library of Ireland, Collection List No. 79: Papers of Patricia Lynch and R. M. Fox. (MS 40, 312/4)

2 Meta Mayne Reid, *The Silver Fighting Cocks* (London: Faber and Faber, 1966)

3   Lynch, *The Kerry Caravan* (London: Dent, 1967), p. 170

4   Letter from Christine Crowley to Patricia Lynch, dated 5 April 1968. National Library of Ireland, Collection List No. 79: Papers of Patricia Lynch and R. M. Fox. (MS 40, 327/2)

5   'Interview with Patricia Lynch', *Ireland of the Welcomes*, September–October 1969. National Library of Ireland, Collection List No. 79: Papers of Patricia Lynch and R. M. Fox. (MS 40, 321)

6   Christine Crowley, *Eirigh*, January 1970

7   Eugene Lambert, 'Recollections of Patricia Lynch', unpublished MS, Special Collection, Saint Patrick's College, Drumcondra, Dublin.

8   Interview with Eugene Lambert conducted by the author, 4 September 2001

9   Lynch, unpublished, undated notes for an obituary of Fox. National Library of Ireland, Collection List No. 79: Papers of Patricia Lynch and R. M. Fox. (MS 40, 309/6)

10 Ibid.

11 Interview with Eugene Lambert conducted by the author, 4 September 2001

12 Letter from Micheál Mac Liammóir to Patricia Lynch, dated 18 March 1970. National Library of Ireland, Collection List No. 79: Papers of Patricia Lynch and R. M. Fox. (MS 40, 327/10)

13 Letter from Patricia Lynch to Eileen Lambert, dated 20 September 1970. National Library of Ireland, Collection List No. 79: Papers of Patricia Lynch and R. M. Fox. (MS 40, 327/8)

14 Letter from Patricia Lynch to Eileen Lambert, dated 10 July 1971. National Library of Ireland, Collection List No. 79: Papers of Patricia Lynch and R. M. Fox (MS 40, 327/8)

15 Interview with Eugene Lambert conducted by the author, 4 September 2001

16 Letter from Patricia Lynch to Eugene and Mai Lambert, undated. National Library of Ireland, Collection List No. 79: Papers of Patricia Lynch and R. M. Fox. (MS 40, 327/8)

17 Robert Dunbar, op. cit., p. 22.

18 Copy of Patricia Lynch's death certificate, National Library of Ireland, Collection List No. 79: Papers of Patricia Lynch and R. M. Fox (MS 40, 334/1)

PART THREE

THE LEGACY OF PATRICIA LYNCH

1   Lynch, *Tales of Irish Enchantment* (Cork: Mercier Press, 1993), p. 36
2   Quote from unpublished lecture delivered by Dr Tom Mullins of UCC Education Department on 19 December 1998. Given to the author by Dr Mullins in February 2002.
3   Lynch, *King of the Tinkers*, p. 62.
4   Lynch, 'Writing for Children', the *Journal of the National Book League*, No. 302, June 1956
5   C. S. Lewis, *On Stories and Other Essays on Literature*, Walter Hooper (ed.) (New York: Harcourt Brace Jovanovich Publishers, 1966), p. 42
6   Lynch, *The Black Goat of Slievemore* (London: Dent, 1959), p. 158
7   Margaret and Michael Rustin, *Narratives of Love and Loss: Studies in Modern Children's Fiction* (London: Kerso, 1987), p. 11
8   Robert Dunbar, *Secret Lands*, p. 18.
9   Francis Spufford, *The Child That Books Built: A Memoir of Childhood and Reading* (London: Faber and Faber, 2002), p. 82
10 Patricia Lynch, *Fiddler's Quest*, p. 13.
11 Declan Kiberd, *Inventing Ireland* (London: Vintage, 1996) p. 268.

IMAGES

1   Lynch, *King of the Tinkers*, p. 110.
2   Charles C. Abbot, *Howard Pyle: A Chronicle* (New York: Harper, 1925), p. 131

BIBLIOGRAPHY

WORKS BY PATRICIA LYNCH

FOR CHILDREN

The Green Dragon (London: Harrap, 1925)

The Turf-Cutter's Donkey (London: Dent, 1934 and New York: Dutton, 1935)

The Turf-Cutter's Donkey Goes Visiting (London: Dent, 1935 and, as *The Donkey Goes Visiting,* New York: Dutton, 1936)

King of the Tinkers (London: Dent, 1938 and New York: Dutton, 1938)

The Turf-Cutter's Donkey Kicks Up His Heels (New York: Dutton, 1939 and London: Dent, 1952)

The Grey Goose of Kilnevin (London: Dent, 1939 and New York: Dutton, 1940)

Fiddler's Quest (London: Dent, 1941 and New York: Dutton, 1943)

Long Ears: The Story of a Little Grey Donkey (London: Dent, 1943)

Strangers at the Fair and Other Stories (Dublin: Browne & Nolan, 1945 and London: Penguin, 1949)

Lisheen at the Valley Farm & Other Stories (Dublin: Gayfield Press, 1945)

The Cobbler's Apprentice (London: Hollis & Carter, 1947)

Brogeen of the Stepping Stones (London: Kerr Cross, 1947)

The Mad O'Haras (London: Dent, 1948 and, as *Grania of Castle O'Hara,* Boston: Page, 1952)

The Dark Sailor of Youghal (London: Dent, 1951)

The Boy at the Swinging Lantern (London: Dent, 1952)

Brogeen Follows the Magic Tune (London: Burke, 1952 and New York: Macmillan, 1968)

Delia Daly of Galloping Green (London: Dent, 1953)

Brogeen and the Green Shoes (London: Burke, 1953)

Brogeen and the Bronze Lizard (London: Burke, 1954 and New York: Macmillan, 1970)

Orla of Burren (London: Dent, 1954)

Tinker Boy (London: Dent, 1955)

Brogeen and the Princess of Sheen (London: Burke, 1955)

The Bookshop on the Quay (London: Dent, 1956)

Brogeen and the Lost Castle (London: Burke, 1956)

Fiona Leaps the Bonfire (London: Dent, 1957)

Cobbler's Luck (London: Burke, 1957)

The Old Black Sea Chest: A Story of Bantry Bay (London: Dent, 1958)

Brogeen and the Black Enchanter (London: Burke, 1958)

The Stone House at Kilgobbin (London: Burke, 1959)

Jinny the Changeling (London: Dent, 1959)

The Runaways (Oxford: Blackwell, 1959)

Sally from Cork (London: Dent, 1960)

The Lost Fisherman of Carrigmor (London: Burke, 1960)

Ryan's Fort (London: Dent, 1961)

The Longest Way Round (London: Burke, 1961)

The Golden Caddy (London: Dent, 1962)

Brogeen and the Little Wind (London: Burke, 1962)

The House by Lough Neagh (London: Dent, 1963)

Brogeen and the Red Fez (London: Burke, 1963)

Holiday at Rosquin (London: Dent, 1964)

Guests at the Beech Tree (London: Burke, 1964)

The Twisted Key and Other Stories (London: Harrap, 1964)

Mona of the Isle (London: Dent, 1965)

Back of Beyond (London: Dent, 1966)

The Kerry Caravan (London: Dent, 1967)

FOR ADULTS

Knights of God: Stories of the Irish Saints (London: Hollis & Carter, 1945 and Chicago: Regnery, 1955)

A Story-Teller's Childhood (London: Dent, 1947)

The Seventh Pig and Other Irish Fairy Tales (London: Dent, 1950); revised edition, *The Black Goat of Slievemore and other Irish Tales* (London: Dent, 1959)

Tales of Irish Enchantment (Dublin: Clonmore & Reynolds and London: Burns & Oates, 1952)

Acc. 4937, Collection List No. 79. Lynch, Patricia and R. M. Fox. Dublin: National Library of Ireland.

Burke, Angela. *The Burning of Bridget Cleary*. London: Pimlico, 1999.

Coghlan, Valerie and Celia Keenan (eds.). *The Big Guide to Irish Children's Books*. Dublin: The Irish Children's Book Trust, 1996.

Donlon, Pat. 'Artful Books: Illustration in Irish Children's Books'. *The Lion and the Unicorn,* Vol. 21, No. 3, 1997.

Dunbar, Robert. 'Barely Pure and Never Simple: The World of Irish Children's Literature'. *The Lion and the Unicorn,* Vol. 21, No. 3, 1997.

———. *Enchanted Journeys*. Dublin: O'Brien Press, 1997.

———. *Secret Lands: The World of Patricia Lynch*. Dublin: O'Brien Press, 1998.

Eccleshare, Julia. *Beatrix Potter to Harry Potter: Portraits of Children's Writers*. London: National Portrait Gallery Publications, 2002.

Fallis, Richard. *The Irish Renaissance*. Dublin: Gill & Macmillan, 1978.

Fallon, Brian. *An Age of Innocence: Irish Culture 1930–1960*. Dublin: Gill & Macmillan, 1968.

Fortnum, Peggy. *Running Wild: Childhood Memories*. London: Chatto and Windus, 1979.

Foster, R. F. *Modern Ireland, 1600–1972*. London: Penguin, 1989.

———. *The Irish Story*. London: Penguin Press, 2001.

Fox, R. M. *Smoky Crusade*. London: Kimble and Bradford, 1937.

———. *China Diary*. London: Robert Hale, 1959.

———. 'Marooned in Venice'. *Irish Independent,* Dublin, 8 August 1967.

Gibbings, Robert. *Lovely is the Lee*. London: Dent, 1945.

———. *Sweet Cork of Thee*. New York: Dutton, 1951.

Havilland, Virginia. *Children and Literature: Views and Reviews*. London: Bodley Head, 1974.

Jeffares, A. Norman. *Anglo-Irish Literature*. London: Macmillan, 1982.

Junior Bookshelf. Special Patricia Lynch Tribute Edition, London, 1943.

Kavanagh, P. J. *Voices in Ireland*. London: John Murray, 1994.

Kennedy, Brian. *Elizabeth Rivers: A Retrospective View*. Dublin: Gorry Gallery, 1989.

Kiberd, Declan. *Inventing Ireland.* London: Vintage, 1996.

Lewis, C. S. *On Stories and Other Essays on Literature.* Walter Hooper (ed.).New York: Harcourt Brace Jovanovich Publishers, 1966.

———. *On Stories: Of Other Words.* Walter Hooper (ed.). London: Geoggrief Bliu, 1966.

Lockhead, Marion. *The Renaissance of Wonder in Children's Literature.* Edinburgh: Canongate, 1977.

Lynch, Patricia. *Garda Review.* Dublin: contributions to various issues, 1945–64.

———. 'Getting the News Across'. *Irish Press,* Dublin, 17 April 1936.

———. 'My Ireland'. *Ireland of the Welcomes.* Dublin, Vol. 18, No. 3, September–October 1969.

———. Short stories in *RTÉ Guide* magazine. Dublin, 20 December 1968 and 23 May 1969.

———. 'Turf and the Tinkers'. *The Cross.* Vol. XXXIII, May 1942.

———. 'Writing for Children'. *Books: The Journal of the National Book League,* No. 302, June 1956.

McDonagh, Michael. 'Origins of the Travelling People' in *Travellers: Citizens of Ireland,* ed. Erica Sheehan, compiled by Frank Murphy, C. M. and Cathleen McDonagh. Dublin: The Parish of the Travelling People, 2000.

MacRaois, Cormac. 'Old Tales for New People: Irish Mythology Retold for Children'. *The Lion and the Unicorn,* Vol. 21, No. 3, 1997.

Mullins, Tom, 'The Eye of Innocence'. Unpublished lecture delivered on 19 December 1998, Cork.

O'Connor, Frank. *The Lonely Voice.* London: Macmillan and Co., 1963.

O'Faoláin, Eileen. *Children of the Salmon.* Dublin: Ward River Press, 1984.

Rustin, Margaret and Michael. *Narratives of Love and Loss: Studies in Modern Children's Fiction.* London: Kerso, 1987.

Scott, Michael, 'By Imagination We Live: Some Thoughts on Irish Children's Fantasy'. *The Lion and the Unicorn,* Vol. 21 No. 3, 1997.

Smyth, Hazel P., *The B. and I. Line: A History of the British and Irish Steam Packet Company.* Dublin: Gill and Macmillan, 1984.

Snoddy, Theo. *Dictionary of Irish Artists: 20th Century.* Dublin: Wolfhound Press, 1966.

Somerville, E. O. and V. M. Ross. *Through Connemara in a Governess Cart.* London: Virago, 1990.

Spufford, Francis. *The Child That Books Built: A Memoir of Childhood and Reading.* London: Faber and Faber, 2002.

Synge, J. M. *Collected Works II: Prose,* (ed.) Robin Skelton. Gerards Cross, Bucks., UK: Colin Smythe, 1982.

Tolkien, J. R. R. *'On Fairy Stories' Tree and Leaf.* London: Geo. Allen and Unwin Ltd., 1964.

Watson, Nancy. 'A Revealing and Exciting Experience: Three of Patricia Lynch's Children's Novels'. *The Lion and the Unicorn,* Vol. 21, No. 3, 1997.

INDEX

197